# The Bible Marksman

A Course in Bible - Marking, covering, in
a simple and comprehensive system, the
most important Bible topics, and
comprising work for one year

By Amos R. Wells

Author of "A Bible Year," etc.

*First Fruits Press*
*Wilmore, Kentucky*
*c2015*

*The Bible marksman: a course in Bible-marking*, by Amos R. Wells.

First Fruits Press, ©2015
Previously published: Boston and Chicago: United Society of Christian Endeavor, ©1900.

ISBN: 9781621714071 (print), 9781621714088 (digital)

Digital version at http://place.asburyseminary.edu/christianendeavorbooks/17/

For all other uses, contact:

First Fruits Press
B.L. Fisher Library
Asbury Theological Seminary
204 N. Lexington Ave.
Wilmore, KY 40390
http://place.asburyseminary.edu/firstfruits

Wells, Amos R. (Amos Russel), 1862-1933.
    The Bible marksman : a course in Bible-marking / by Amos R. Wells.
    124 pages ; 21 cm.
    Wilmore, Ky. : First Fruits Press, ©2015.
    Includes index.
    "Covering, in a simple and comprehensive system, the most important Bible topics, and comprising work for one year."
    Reprint. Previously published: Boston : United Society of Christian Endeavor, ©1900.
    ISBN: 9781621714071 (pbk.)
    1. Bible – Reading. 2. Bible – Study and teaching. I. Title.
BS617 .W44 2015

Cover design by Jonathan Ramsay

asburyseminary.edu
800.2ASBURY
204 North Lexington Avenue
Wilmore, Kentucky 40390

*First Fruits*
THE ACADEMIC OPEN PRESS OF ASBURY SEMINARY

First Fruits Press

*The Academic Open Press of Asbury Theological Seminary*

204 N. Lexington Ave., Wilmore, KY 40390

859-858-2236

first.fruits@asburyseminary.edu

asbury.to/firstfruits

# The Bible Marksman

A Course in Bible-Marking,

covering, in a simple and comprehensive system, the most important Bible topics, and comprising work for one year

## By Amos R. Wells
### Author of "A Bible Year," etc.

United Society of Christian Endeavor
Boston and Chicago

# PREFACE.

THE following course in Bible-marking was pursued, during its first appearance in *The Christian Endeavor World*, by more than three thousand registered "Bible Marksmen." Among these were many busy pastors, some of whom could find time for this work only by rising in the small hours of the morning. Many others were earnest Sunday-school teachers, whose classes were enthusiastic over this practical method of gaining familiarity with the Book of Books. The superintendents of Junior Christian Endeavor societies found the course well within the understanding of their young charges. In fact, the ages of those following the course ranged, so far as is known, from five to eighty-six.

Mothers marked Bibles for their sons to use when they should be able to read. Classes were formed in homes. Other classes, led by pastors, were formed in Christian Endeavor societies. The Y. M. C. A., the Epworth League, and other organizations, found it useful to some of their members. The plan was utilized in family prayers. Some enthusiasts copied the entire course for others that could not take the paper. One missionary even proposes to translate the course into Chinese!

3

Moreover, Marksmen reported themselves from many distant regions of the earth—from South Africa, Canada, Japan. Mexico, Turkey, England, Jamaica, Cuba, China, New Zealand, and even a class of twenty-two in Palestine, nearly all of whom did their marking in Arabic Bibles.

Since the course has met with such a reception, it has been thought likely that many may wish to have it in permanent form, more especially as, so far as the author knows, no system of Bible-marking, at the same time simple and comprehensive, has ever before been printed.

It is believed that familiarity with this method will give great facility not only in marking the Bible, but in using it after it is marked. Fifteen minutes will easily suffice to accomplish the work here laid down for any day, and is not that small fraction of time well bestowed if it will acquaint us with a great Bible truth, and place it where our hands can readily find it if our memory at any time proves treacherous?

AMOS R. WELLS.

*Boston.*

4

# CONTENTS.

# THE BIBLE MARKSMAN.

## DIRECTIONS FOR BIBLE-MARKING.

This course in Bible-marking has been made as simple as possible. The simpler the method, the clearer it is, and the more likely it is to be followed throughout life. The materials should be readily accessible, and therefore we shall dispense with colored inks, carefully ruled lines, and elaborate symbols. We shall use black ink and an ordinary pen.

It is not well to underscore, except for emphasis, of which underscoring is the natural sign. The place for Bible-marking is the margin, where the marks are most easily seen, and where they will not confuse the eye.

The most obvious symbols for Bible-marking are letters, and those we shall use in this course. The chief topics will be represented by single letters,—" F " for faith, and so on. The less important topics under each letter will be represented by two letters,—" Fg " for forgiveness, etc. The second letter is to come from the accented syllable of the word, if possible.

One great subject is chosen for each week. Thus in the course of the year all the important topics of the Bible, and most of the less important teachings, are systematically covered and mapped out. At the close of the year the system may, of course, be extended to other topics.

Scarcely any subject can be exhaustively considered; this is especially true of the supreme subjects with which the course opens. Only the

7

principal texts can be given, with the expectation that later reading will add others.

The theme for each week is divided into seven sub-topics, illustrated by the chief passages that bear on the subject. These are numbered,—(F1, F2, F3, etc.,)—and each is carried on by a list of texts running through the Bible. It is the expectation that the careful reading and meditation will be spent only upon the first passage for each day, the remaining passages being read less carefully and marked as they are read.

To prepare your Bible for marking, first number the pages of the New Testament consecutively with those of the Old, if they are not so numbered already, and insert in the back of the book several pages of firm, thin paper. Upon these pages will be written, in order, the week's subject and sub-topics, with the seven initial texts for each week, or, if preferred, the page on which each is found. These will guide you at any time to the beginnings of the seven chains of texts under each topic. Taking as an example the first sub-topic of the first week, "God is almighty," turn to its reference, Isa. 40: 12–26, and write "G1" in the margin. The first text to be linked with it in the chain is 1 Chron. 29: 11, 12, which (in my Bible) is on page 448. I therefore place 448 below G1, thus: $_{448}^{G1}$. Turning now to 1 Chron. 29: 11, 12, write G1 in the margin; see that the next text, Job 38: 4, is on page 553, and complete the sign opposite 1 Chron. 29: 11, 12, making it $_{553}^{G1}$. Thus proceed, taking each day a fresh start on a new chain. The last text of each day's chain will be marked simply "G1," or whatever the symbol may be, and later reading may lengthen the chain from this point.

Of course, if a verse is upon two different subjects, it will come to have two marks in the margin. If the entire chapter is on one subject, you can write the symbol opposite the chapter title. To indicate that more than one verse is included, draw a vertical line in the margin from the first to the last, or repeat the symbol, making the reference to the next text only with the last verse. It is still better, probably, to include the whole in a symbol opposite the first verse. Thus, if you want to indicate under J2 the reference, 2 Cor. 3:8, 13–15, write "J2" opposite 2 Cor. 3:8, add beneath it "vs. 13–15" or simply "13–15," and beneath that the next page number.

Some prefer to link the last text of each sub-topic to the leading text of the next sub-topic, joining the last text of all to the first for the week, thus binding the chain together. Some place the *last* page above each symbol as well as the *next* page below it, thus being able to read either forward or backward. Some write the sub-topic number as an exponent, thus: Fg². Some indicate the leading texts by circles around their symbols. Some find it more convenient to begin marking at the end of each chain, thus working forward. Some do the marking for the entire week on one day, that for the rest of the week they may use these markings in reading and meditation. Some prefer an indelible pencil to ink. Some write the leading texts in a notebook instead of the backs of their Bibles, leaving space each week for original comments. Many variations such as these have been brought to my attention; and, indeed, the plan is so simple as to lend itself easily to whatever modifications the taste or circumstances of the Bible-reader may suggest.

I desire to urge upon all beginners in Bible-marking the purchase of a Revised Bible, with good type, firm paper, and large margins.

# The First Week.

## GOD.

### (Symbol, G.)

### Sub-Topics and Leading Texts.

January 1.—*God is almighty.* Isa. 40:12-26. (G 1.)
January 2.—*God is all-wise.* Rom. 11:33-36. (G 2.)
January 3.—*God is everywhere.* Ps. 139:7-10. (G 3.)
January 4.—*God is glorious.* Ps. 24:7-10. (G 4.)
January 5.—*God is just.* Deut. 32:4. (G 5.)
January 6.—*God is good.* Nah. 1:7. (G 6.)
January 7.—*God is love.* John 3:16. (G 7.)

### Texts to be Linked with the Principal Ones.

January 1.—(G 1.)—1 Chron. 29:11, 12; Job 38:4-7; Ps. 24:1, 2; 104:1-5; Isa. 26:4; 64:8; Jer. 27:5; Amos 5:8; Nah. 1:3-6; Hab. 3:3-15; Rev. 19:6.

January 2.—(G 2.)—Ps. 33:11; 94:9; 104:24; Prov. 3:19, 20; Eccl. 3:14; Isa. 55:8, 9; Jas. 1:17.

January 3.—(G 3.)—Gen. 28:16; Josh. 1:9; 2 Chron. 15:2; Job 23:3; Isa. 57:15; Jer. 23:23, 24; Acts 17:24-28.

January 4.—(G 4.)—Ex. 33:20-22; Ps. 8:1; 19:1; 46:10; 96:1-8; 145:10-12; Isa. 2:10; 6:1-3; Ezek. 43:2; 1 Tim. 6:15, 16; Rev. 4:11.

January 5.—(G 5.)—Num. 23:19; 2 Sam. 22:26, 27; 2 Chron. 19:7; Neh. 9:33; Job 4:17; Ps. 19:9; 103:6; Ezek. 18:25; Rom. 3:26; Rev. 15:3.

January 6.—(G. 6.)—1 Sam. 12:22; Ps. 34:8; 36:5, 7; 84:11; 145:7; Prov. 10:22; Lam. 3:25.

January 7.—(G. 7.)—Ex. 19:4; Deut. 7:7, 8; 33: 12; Ps. 63:3; 103:4; Isa. 66:13; Hos. 11:1, 4; John 14:21, 23; 16:27; 17:23–26; Rom. 5:8; Eph. 2:4; 1 John 3:1; 4:9, 10, 16, 19.

### For Meditation throughout the Week.

Since Thou art so powerful, O my God, and since all Thy power is ready to help me, how can I tremble and be afraid! Thy plans cannot be anything but the best plans, and I will submit my will to Thine. Thou canst have no desire except for my happiness, my joy being Thy joy, dear Father; let me remember this when life seems hard. And Thou art here; with all Thy majesty and love, Thou art beside me now. God, Father, show me Thyself. Let me make Thy glory my one ambition, Thy wisdom my sole guidance, Thy power my only reliance. By study of Thy Word, by long and eager meditation, and by the grace of Thy Holy Spirit, I would acquaint myself with Thee. Knowing Thee, I shall know my happiness and my salvation, forever and ever,

# The Second Week.

## CHRIST.

(Symbol, X, the first letter of the Greek word for Christ.)

### Sub-Topics and Leading Texts.

January 8.—*Prophecies of Christ.* Isa. 53:4–12. (X 1.)

January 9.—*His divinity.* John 1:1–5, 18, 34. (X 2.)

January 10.—*His character.* Heb. 12:2. (X 3.)

January 11.—*His mission.* Matt. 20:28. (X 4.)

January 12.—*His authority.* Phil. 2:9–11. (X 5.)

January 13.—*His love.* John 15:9–15. (X 6.)

January 14.—*His atonement.* John 3:14, 15. (X 7.)

### Texts to be Linked with the Principal Ones.

January 8.—(X 1.)—Gen. 3:15; 12:3; 49:10; Num. 24:17; Deut. 18:15; Job 19:25; Ps. 2:6–9; 22:18; 69:7–9, 21; 72:2–17; 110:1; Isa. 9:6, 7; 11:1–10; 32:2; 40:9–11; 42:1–7; 52:13, 14; 61:1–3; 63:1–9; Jer. 23:5, 6; Ezek. 34:23; Dan. 2:35, 44; 7:13, 14; Mic. 5:2; Zech. 9:9, 10; 13:1; Mal. 3:1–3; 4:2.

January 9.—(X 2.)—Matt. 12:41, 42; 26:63, 64; Luke 22:70; 24:25–27; John 5:17, 18, 23; 6:54, 62; 8:23, 28, 56–58; 10:30–38; 13:19; 14:6, 11, 19; 17:5; 2 Cor. 5:19; Col. 2:9.

January 10.—(X 3.)—Matt. 11:27, 29; 26:39; Luke 2:49; 22:27; John 4:34; 5:30, 34; 7:46; 8:29, 46, 55; 9:4; 13:14; Rom. 15:3; 2 Cor. 8:9; Heb. 4:14, 15.

January 11.—(X 4.)—Luke 5:32; 19:10; John 3:17; 6:38; 10:10, 11, 15; 14:2; Acts 5:31; Rom. 14:9; Gal. 1:3, 4.

12

January 12.—(X 5.)—Matt. 7:29; 8:27; 12:6,8; 13:
41; 23:10; 25:31-33; 28:18; Luke 10:22;
22:29; John 3:35; 5:21-23, 27; 13:13; 18:
37; Eph. 1:22; Rev. 3:7; 19:11-16.

January 13.—(X 6.)—Matt. 9:36; 18:6, 10; 23:37;
Mark 9:36, 37; 10:16, 21; John 11:5, 35,
36; 13:1, 23, 34; 14:21; 17:9, 11, 20; Rom.
8:35-39; Gal. 2:20; Eph. 3:18, 19; 5:2,
25; Rev. 1:5.

January 14.—(X 7.)—Matt. 1:21; 26:28; John 1:
29; 6:51; Acts 4:12; Rom. 4:25; 5:6-11;
1 Cor. 3:11; 2 Cor. 5:21; Col. 1:14-22;
1 Tim. 1:15; 1 Pet. 1:18, 19; 2:24; 1 John
1:7; 2:2; Rev. 5:9.

## For Meditation throughout the Week.

" Thou, O Christ, art all I want." Every need,
of body or soul, finds in Thee its supreme satisfaction. Every ambition that is worth cherishing
for a moment is eternally fulfilled in Thee. Out
of my restless, burdened life I turn to Thee for
peace, sure that I shall find it. From the midst of
whirling perplexities, the dust and darkness of
this world, I stretch a groping hand and it touches
Thine; Thou wilt draw me out of it all, into a
place of perfect calm and unalloyed happiness.
Why do I ever forget Thee? Why do I ever walk
alone? Why do I ever choose misery for joy and
the world for heaven? Forgive me, merciful
Saviour, and save me, daily and hourly, from myself to Thee. Amen.

# The Third Week.

## THE HOLY SPIRIT.

### (Symbol, H S.)

### Sub-Topics and Leading Texts.

January 15.—*The Holy Trinity.* 1 John 5:6-8. (H S 1.)

January 16.—*Names of the Holy Spirit.* 1 Pet. 4: 14. (H S 2.)

January 17.—*The Holy Spirit in the Old Testament.* Zech. 4:6. (H S 3.)

January 18.—*Sins against the Holy Spirit.* Eph. 4:30. (H S 4.)

January 19.—*The Holy Spirit and Prayer.* Rom. 8:26, 27. (H S 5.)

January 20.—*The Teacher and Transformer.* John 14:26. (H S 6.)

January 21. — *The Comforter.* Eph. 3:14-16. (H S 7.)

### Texts to be Linked with the Principal Ones.

January 15.—(H S 1.)—Matt. 28:19; Luke 1:35; John 20:22; Acts 5:32; 2 Cor. 13:14; Eph. 2:18, 22; Rev. 22:17.

January 16.—(H S 2.)—John 15:26; Rom. 8:9; Gal. 4:6; 1 Thess. 4:8; Heb. 9:14; 10:29; 1 Pet. 1:11, 12; Rev. 4:5.

January 17.—(H S 3.)—Gen. 1:2; 6:3; Ex. 31:1-3; Num. 27:18; Judg. 6:34; Neh. 9:20, 30; Job 33:4; Ps. 51:11, 12; Isa. 32:15; 40:13; 44:3; Ezek. 11:5, 24; Joel 2:28; Mic. 2:7; Zech. 12:10.

January 18.—(H S 4.)—Matt. 12:31, 32; Mark 3:28, 29; Acts 5:3, 4; 7:51; 8:18-20; 1 Thess. 5:19; Heb. 10:29.

January 19.—(H S 5.)—Zech. 12:10; Luke 11:13; Acts 4:31; Eph. 2:18; 6:18; Jude 20.

January 20.—(H S 6.)—Luke 12:12; John 3:5-8; 16:13, 14; Acts 2:4, 38; 8:29, 39; Rom. 8:2, 11, 14, 16; 1 Cor. 2:4, 9-14; 3:16; 12:4-11; 2 Cor. 3:17, 18; Gal. 5:16-25; 2 Pet. 1:21; Rev. 2:7.

January 21.—(H S 7.)—John 14:16, 17; 16:7; Acts 9:31; Rom. 14:17; 15:13, 30; Gal. 6:8; Eph. 4:3; 5:18.

## For Meditation throughout the Week.

Oh, to know Thee better, Infinite Being! I have been ignobly content to know so little of Thee, to know Thee in so few relations, to apprehend so few of the glories of Thy character. I would enter into the mystery of the Holy Trinity. Knowing Thee as the Father and the Son, I would go on to know Thee as the Holy Spirit. O Thou teaching One, guide me daily into fresh realms of truth. O Thou transforming One, grant me the new birth into Thy purity and power. O Thou blessed Comforter, make all my sorrows joyous with the shining of Thy presence, the soothing of Thy love. I cannot know Thee wholly. After endless ages of thought and vision, I could not know Thee wholly. I will bless Thee for Thy gracious disclosures, and I will be certain that Thou wilt ever show me more and more, as I press toward Thee with a sincere heart.

# The Fourth Week.

## WORSHIP.

### (Symbol, W.)

### Sub-Topics and Leading Texts.

January 22.—*The duty of worship.* Ps. 96:9. (W 1.)

January 23.—*The joy of worship.* Ps. 84:1-10. (W 2.)

January 24.—*The rewards of worship.* Isa. 40:27 -31. (W 3.)

January 25.—*True worship.* John 4:23, 24. (W 4.)

January 26.—*False worship.* Matt. 15:7-9. (W 5.)

January 27.—*Examples of worship in the Old Testament.* Ex. 20:24. (W 6.)

January 28.—*Examples of worship in the New Testament.* Rev. 5:11-14. (W 7.)

### Texts to be Linked with the Principal Ones.

January 22.—(W 1.)—Lev. 19:30; Deut. 6:13; Ps. 95:6, 7; 97:7; 99:5; Isa. 12:6; 17:7; Heb. 10:25; Rev. 14:7; 15:4.

January 23.—(W 2.)—1 Chron. 29:3; Ps. 26:8; 27:4; 63:1, 2; 122:1.

January 24.—(W 3.)—Ps. 27:5, 14; 36:8; 65:4; 73:2, 3, 17; 92:13, 14; Isa. 2:3; 56:6, 7.

January 25.—(W 4.)—Gen. 35:2, 3; Ex. 3:5; Job 1:19-21; Ps. 5:7; 26:6, 7; 29:2; 55:14; 66:13, 14; Eccl. 5:1, 2; Amos 5:23, 24; Matt. 5:23, 24; 18:20; Acts 2:1.

January 26.—(W 5.)—Lev. 10:1, 2; Num. 16:35; 1 Sam. 2:12-17; 6:19; 13:9-14; 2 Sam. 6:6, 7; 2 Kings 21:7; 2 Chron. 26:16-21; 28:24; Dan. 3:6; Matt. 4:8, 9; 2 Thess. 2:4.

January 27.—(W 6.)—Gen. 21:33; 35:1, 14, 15;
      Deut. 12:5; 26:10, 11; Josh. 18:1; 2
      Chron. 5:13, 14; Ezra 3:11-13; Neh. 8:9,
      10; Joel 2:15-17; Zech. 14:17.
January 28.—(W 7.)—Luke 2:41; 4:16; Acts 1:14;
      2:1, 42, 46, 47; 4:23-31; 12:12; 16:13-15.

## For Meditation throughout the Week.

There is no condescension like this, that I, so insignificant and so sinful, am admitted into the presence of God. Why am I not overpowered when I enter His house, or bow before Him in my closet? Why does not my heart fail me through awe of His glory? Why do I not sink with the shame of my sins? Is it because I am heedless and ignorant, neither knowing nor caring to know in what Presence I stand? Or is it because I am bold with the confidence Thou alone canst give me, loving Intercessor, my Elder Brother? It is both, O Christ, now one and now the other, now drunken with my follies, touching with irreverent hand the ark of God, and now approaching the Throne with glad courage, because Thou dost hold my hand. Grant that this true worship may alone be mine henceforth, O Thou through whom alone men go to God. Amen.

# The Fifth Week.

## THE SABBATH.

### (Symbol, Sb.)

### Sub-Topics and Leading Texts.

January 29.—*The Sabbath law.* Ex. 20: 8–11. (Sb 1.)

January 30.—*Examples of Sabbath-keeping.* Exod. 16: 5, 22–30. (Sb 2.)

January 31.—*Sabbath joy.* Ps. 118: 24. (Sb 3.)

February 1.—*Sabbath rewards.* Isa. 58: 13, 14. (Sb 4.)

February 2.—*The Pharisee's Sabbath.* Matt. 12: 1–14. (Sb 5.)

February 3.—*Sabbath warnings.* Ezek. 20: 12–21. (Sb 6.)

February 4.—*Sabbath reforms.* Neh. 13: 15–22. (Sb 7.)

### Texts to be Linked with the Principal Ones.

January 29.—(Sb 1.)—Gen. 2: 1–3; Ex. 23: 10–12; 31: 12–17; 34: 21; 35: 2, 3; Lev. 19: 30; 23: 3; Num. 15: 32–36; Deut. 5: 12–15; Isa. 66: 23; Mark 2: 27, 28.

January 30.—(Sb 2.)—Lev. 26: 34, 35; Ezek. 46: 1, 3; Mark 3: 1–6; 6: 2; Luke 4: 16, 31; 13: 14–17; 14: 1–6; 23: 56; Acts 13: 44; 16: 13; 1 Cor. 16: 2; Rev. 1: 10.

January 31.—(Sb 3.)—Isa. 56: 2, 6, 7.

February 1.—(Sb 4.)—Jer. 17: 21–27; Heb. 4: 4, 9.

February 2.—(Sb 5.)—Isa. 1: 13; Amos 8: 5.

February 3.—(Sb 6.)—Ezek. 22:8; 23:38; Hos. 2:
11.
February 4.—(Sb 7.)—Neh. 9:13, 14; 10:29–31; Lam.
2:5, 6; John 7:19–24.

## For Meditation throughout the Week.

Let me rise into the thought of God, and that
clear atmosphere will quiet all the fever of this
world, and hush my spirit with a glad reverence,
so that every day will be a Sabbath day to me.
And when thus every day has become a Sabbath,
I shall wish, with tenfold my present desire, to
spend one day in seven wholly in God's praise
and direct service. What artifice, what self-deception, what hypocrisy, attend my Sabbath-
keeping! How I strive to trick my conscience, to
smuggle worldliness into the sacred hours, to
cheat myself to my eternal hurt! Let me no
longer juggle with the Lord's day. It is His
entirely, as I am His entirely. Shall He not do
what He will with His own? As I enter upon it
I will ask, "Lord, what wilt Thou have me to do?"
As each hour arrives I will ask, "Lord, how shall
I fill this hour?" And at the close I shall bow
before Thee in great joy, and thank Thee for the
best day I have ever lived.

# The Sixth Week.

## THE BIBLE.

### (Symbol, B.)

### Sub-Topics and Leading Texts.

February 5.—*The Bible's wisdom.* Ps. 119:18, 98-100, 104, 105, 130. (B 1.)

February 6.—*The Bible's authority.* Heb. 4:12. (B 2.)

February 7.—*The Bible's inspiration.* 2 Tim. 3:16, 17. (B 3.)

February 8.—*The Bible loved.* Jer. 15:16. (B 4.)

February 9.—*The Bible misused and rejected.* Jer. 8:9. (B 5.)

February 10.—*The Bible rightly used.* Deut. 6:6-9. (B 6.)

February 11.—*Bible benefits.* Josh. 1:8. (B 7.)

### Texts to be Linked with the Principal Ones.

February 5.—(B 1.)—Deut. 4:6; Ps. 19:7, 8; 94:12; 147:15; Mark 12:24; 2 Tim. 3:15.

February 6.—(B 2.)—Deut. 4:8-10; 12:32; 17:18,19; Ps. 12:6; 18:30; Isa. 40:8; 55:10,11; Jer. 13:15; 22:29; 23:28, 29; 2 Tim. 2:9.

February 7.—(B 3.)—Ex. 24:12; Num. 33:2; Deut. 4:5; Ps. 147:19; Isa. 59:21; Jer. 36:2; Ezek. 11:25; Matt. 22:31; Luke 1:70; Acts 28:25; Rom. 3:2; 1 Cor. 2:12; Heb. 1:1; 2 Pet. 1:21; 1 John 1:5; Rev. 1:1, 2; 19:10.

February 8.—(B 4.)—Deut. 32:46; Job 23:12; Ps. 1:2; 19:10; 40:8; 119:14-16, 24, 97, 103, 140, 162; Ezek. 3:3, 10.

February 9.—(B 5.)—Ps. 50:17; Prov. 13:13; 30:6; Isa. 5:24; Jer. 23:36; 36:1–32; Matt. 15: 3; Luke 16:31; John 5:46, 47; 1 Pet. 2:8; 2 Pet. 3:16; Rev. 22:18, 19.

February 10.—(B 6.)—Deut. 30:11-14; Ps. 119:11; Hab. 2:2; Matt. 7:24, 25; 11:15; Luke 11:28; John 5:39; 20:31; Acts 17:11; Eph. 6:17; 2 Tim. 2:15; Jas. 1:21-25.

February 11.—(B 7.)—Neh. 9:29; Ps. 19:11; 37:31; 119:9, 50, 165; Mic. 2:7; Matt. 13:23; Acts 20:32; Rom. 10:17; 15:4; Jas. 1:21; 1 Pet. 2:2.

## For Meditation throughout the Week.

Here is the record of God's dealings with the people that have been truest to Him. How am I using it to strengthen my loyalty? Here are God's revelations to the minds that have been most open to Him. How am I using it to see into the eternal realities? Here are God's warnings, illustrated in history and uttered by His prophets. How am I purifying my life with them? Here are promises, proved unfailing by all souls that have tested them. What comfort, what courage, are they to me? Here, above all, is the nearest way to my Saviour, the vital, breathing record of His words and deeds. Does it breathe throughout my days and shine in my nights? I will no longer neglect the Bible. In deed, now, as always in word, it shall be my most precious possession. Holy Spirit, who didst implant these thoughts in human minds, fix them in my mind also, and may no word return unto Thee void. Amen.

# The Seventh Week.

## THE CHURCH.

### (Symbol, Ch.)

### Sub-Topics and Leading Texts.

February 12.—*The Church's Head.* Col. 1:18.
(Ch 1.)

February 13.—*The Church's glory.* Isa. 62:1.
(Ch 2.)

February 14.—*Church helpfulness.* Rom. 15:1, 2.
(Ch 3.)

February 15.—*Church union.* John 17:11, 21-23.
(Ch 4.)

February 16.—*Church purification.* Gal. 6:1.
(Ch 5.)

February 17.—*Prayer for the Church.* 2 Chron.
6:40, 41. (Ch 6.)

February 18.—*The pastor's authority and duty.*
1 Cor. 4:1. (Ch 7.)

### Texts to be Linked With the Principal Ones.

February 12.—(Ch 1.)—Eph. 1:22, 23; 2:20–22; 4:
15; 5:23; Col. 2:10, 19; 1 Pet. 2:7; Rev.
1:13, 20.

February 13.—(Ch 2.)—Ps. 48:1, 2, 12, 13; 50:2; 87:
3; 1 Tim. 3:15; Heb. 12:22, 23; Rev. 21:2.

February 14.—(Ch 3.)—Ps. 119:63; Mal. 3:16; Luke
22:32; Acts 20:35, Rom. 14:1, 19; Gal. 6:
2; Phil. 4:3; Col. 3:16; 1 Thess. 5:11, 14;
Heb. 3:13; 10:24; Jas. 5:16; 1 John 1:7.

February 15.—(Ch 4.)—John 10:16; Rom. 12:4, 5;
1 Cor. 10:17; 12:5, 12–27; Gal. 3:26–28;
Eph. 4:4–6, 12, 13, 16, 25; Col. 3:11, 15.

February 16.—(Ch 5.)—Matt. 18 : 15–18 ; Rom. 16 : 17 ;
    1 Cor. 5 : 6, 7, 11–13 ; 16 : 22 ; 2 Cor. 2 : 6–11 ;
    6 : 14, 15 ; 2 Thess. 3 : 6, 14, 15 ; 2 Tim. 4 : 2 ;
    Tit. 3 : 10, 11 ; 2 John 10, 11.
February 17.—(Ch 6.)—1 Kings 8 : 28–40 ; Ps. 20 : 1–
    4 ; 51 : 18 ; 80 : 1, 14, 15 ; 122 : 7, 8 ; Dan. 9 :
    17 ; Eph. 3 : 14–19.
February 18.—(Ch 7.)—Mal. 2 : 7 ; Acts 20 : 27, 28 ;
    2 Cor. 8 : 5 ; 1 Thess. 5 : 12, 13 ; 1 Tim. 5 : 17 ;
    Heb. 13 : 7, 17.

## For Meditation throughout the Week.

The Church, which is Thy body! The Church, which is to do what Thy body did, when Thou wert in the tabernacle of the flesh! The Church which, like Thee, is to go about doing good, to lay warm hands upon the lonely, to raise the fallen, to embrace the outcast. The Church which, like Thee, is to have no will but the Father's, and to find its meat and drink in doing His pleasure! I am unworthy to be even the least and lowest member of this, Thy body. I am unworthy to be the ground upon which it treads, the inert material with which it works. Yet Thou hast set me to do the work of Thy hand, Thy tongue, Thy heart. Blessed Lord, Thou who hast chosen me wilt also enable me. Thou wilt draw me up into Thyself. Thou wilt arm me with Thy power and gift me with Thy wisdom. And being at one with Thee, I shall not shrink even from the mighty responsibilities Thou dost lay upon a member of Thy Church.

# The Eighth Week.

## MISSIONS.

### (Symbol, M.)

## Sub-Topics and Leading Texts.

February 19.—*The Great Commission.* Matt. 28: 19, 20. (M 1.)

February 20.—*The scope of missions.* Matt. 6: 10. (M 2.)

February 21.—*The power of missions.* Acts 1: 8. (M 3.)

February 22.—*The success of missions.* Mal. 1: 11. (M 4.)

February 23.—*The missionary appeal.* Acts 16: 9, 10. (M 5.)

February 24.—*The missionary spirit.* Acts 20: 18–24. (M 6.)

February 25.—*Great missionaries.* Acts 13: 2–4. (M 7.)

## Texts to be Linked with the Principal Ones.

February 19.—(M 1.)—Ps. 68: 11; Isa. 40: 3; Matt. 9: 37, 38; 10: 8; Mark 16: 15; Luke 9: 60; 24: 47.

February 20.—(M 2.)—Ps. 2: 8; 33: 8; Isa. 9: 2; 32: 20; Matt. 13: 38; Luke 13: 29; Rom. 15: 20; 1 John 4: 14.

February 21.—(M 3.)—Ex. 4: 12; 2 Chron. 16: 9; Ps. 29: 11; Jer. 1: 19; 1 Cor. 2: 2; 2 Cor. 3: 5.

February 22.—(M 4.)—Ps. 37: 11; Isa. 42: 17; Hag. 2: 7; Zech. 2: 11; John 12: 32; 1 Cor. 3: 6; Phil. 2: 10.

February 23.—(M 5.)—Josh. 13: 1; Esth. 4: 14; Isa. 43: 6; Luke 18: 29, 30; Rom. 10: 14, 15; Jas. 5: 20.

February 24.—(M 6.)—2 Sam. 24:24; 2 Chron. 14:
11; Luke 5:28; 1 Cor. 1:26–29; 2 Cor. 6:
10; Gal. 1:15, 16; 2 Tim. 2:4.
February 25.—(M 7.)—Jer. 1:17; Jonah 3:3; Acts
5:41; 8:4, 35; 10:28; 18:9, 10; Phil. 3:8;
1 Tim. 2:7; Rev. 20:4.

## For Meditation throughout the Week.

Thy kingdom come, dear Lord; Thy kingdom,
which has no room for sighs or tears, for pain or
any woe. Thy will be done, dear Lord; Thy will
of power and of peace. How fast would Thy
kingdom come if all men were like me? How
speedily would Thy will triumph if missions took
their pace from my life? Alas, for my sluggish
will, my coward tongue, my selfish purse! There
in the van are Thy heroes, men and women who
have left all to follow Thee, of whom the world is
not worthy, of whom I am all unworthy. They
trust Thee. They yield their fortunes into Thy
hand. Through Thee they win their victories. In
all lands and on all seas they are busy, driving
back the kingdom of darkness and bringing in
the kingdom of Thy dear Son. I also will trust
Thy word. I also will believe that Thou dost not
forsake Thy servants. I also will leave all and
follow Thee.

# The Ninth Week.

## SIN.

### (Symbol, Sn.)

### Sub-Topics and Leading Texts.

February 26.—*The roots of sin.* Prov. 4:23. (Sn 1.)
February 27.—*The sinner's portrait.* Rom. 1:28-32. (Sn 2.)
February 28. — *Sin's fearful results.* Gal. 6:7. (Sn 3.)
March 1.—*God hates sin.* Deut. 25:16. (Sn 4.)
March 2.—*The Christian's attitude toward sin.* Rom. 7:24. (Sn 5.)
March 3.—*Punishment for sin in the Old Testament.* Ps. 1:4-6. (Sn 6.)
March 4.—*Punishment for sin in the New Testament.* Matt. 25:46. (Sn 7.)

### Texts to be Linked with the Principal Ones.

February 26.—(Sn 1.)—Deut. 29:18; 2 Chron. 12:14; Jer. 17:9; Matt. 12:33-35; 15:19, 20; Heb. 12:15; Jas. 1:14; 1 John 3:8-10.
February 27.—(Sn 2.)—1 Kings 21:20; Job 15:15, 16; Ps. 36:1-4; Prov. 4:16; Isa. 5:18; Jer. 2:22; 4:22; John 8:34, 44; Rom. 8:6-8; Eph. 2:12.
February 28.—(Sn 3.)—Ex. 20:5; Job 4:8; Ps. 9:15, 16; Prov. 1:31; 8:36; 22:8; Isa. 57:20, 21; Jer. 31:30; Hos. 8:7; 10:13.
March 1.—(Sn 4.)—Ps. 5:4-6; 11:5; Prov. 15:9, 26; Hos. 4:1; Hab. 1:13; Luke 16:15.
March 2.—(Sn 5.)—Gen. 39:9; Ps. 26:9; 84:10; 119:104; 139:21, 22; Prov. 8:13; Jer. 9:2; Jude 23.

March 3.—(Sn 6.)—Gen. 4:7; Ex. 32:33, 34; Num.
32:23; Deut. 32:41, 42; Job 11:20; 21:17-
20; Ps. 32:10; 34:16, 21; Prov. 11:21; 14:
12; Eccl. 8:13; Isa. 11:4; Ezek. 18:4;
Mal. 4:1.

March 4.—(Sn 7.)—Matt. 7:23; 15:13; 24:51; Luke
12:5; 20:18; John 5:29; Rom. 6:23; 1 Cor.
3:17; Gal. 3:10; Eph. 5:6; Heb. 10:31;
Jas. 1:15; 1 Pet. 3:12.

## For Meditation throughout the Week.

Why does not God kill the devil? Because He
wants me to! It is His way of strengthening me,
to force my life into conflict. It is His way of
purifying me, conquering, "so as by fire," the
flames of evil passions.

The struggle is enormously difficult. There are
faintings and fears, blows and wounds, tortures
and agonies innumerable. Yes, and there is many
a defeat.

But I will not yield. Nothing shall defeat me.
Though I fall a thousand times, yea, a thousand
thousand, I shall still count myself invincible; for
I shall keep hold on God.

It is God's will that sin shall die; to that strong
will I commit myself and my sins. The blood of
Christ shall wash away all the wounds of my de-
feats. The cross of Christ shall be my barrier
against every onrush of the foe. *I* shall not conquer, but I shall make His conquest mine, by the
faith that knows no refusal, the confidence that
endures and triumphs forever.

# The Tenth Week.

## TEMPTATION.

### (Symbol, Tt.)

### Sub-Topics and Leading Texts.

March 5.—*How God uses temptations.* 1 Cor. 10: 12, 13. (Tt 1.)

March 6.—*Conquering temptation.* Matt. 26:41. (Tt 2.)

March 7.—*Preserved in temptation.* Eph. 6:10-18. (Tt 3.)

March 8.—*Prayer against temptation.* Matt. 6: 13. (Tt 4.)

March 9.—*Gain from temptation.* Jas. 1: 2, 3, 12, 13, 14. (Tt 5.)

March 10.—*Tempting or helping others.* Rom. 14: 13, 15. (Tt 6.)

March 11.—*Lessons from great temptations.* Mark 1: 13. (Tt 7.)

### Texts to be Linked with the Principal Ones.

March 5.—(Tt 1.)—Gen. 22: 1; Ex. 16: 4; Deut. 8: 2; 2 Chron. 32: 31; Job 23: 10; Ps. 103: 14; John 6: 6; Jude 24.

March 6.—(Tt 2.)—Ps. 119: 101; Prov. 1: 10, 15; 4: 14, 15; Matt. 4: 4, 7, 10; 5: 29, 30; 1 Cor. 9: 27; 10: 12; Gal. 5: 16, 17; Heb. 12: 3, 4; Jas. 4: 7; 1 Pet. 5: 8, 9.

March 7.—(Tt 3.)—Ps. 94: 18; 2 Thess. 3: 3; Heb. 2: 18; 4: 15; 2 Pet. 2: 9; 1 John 4: 4; Rev. 3: 10.

March 8.—(Tt 4.)—1 Chron. 4: 10; Ps. 19: 12, 13; 119: 37; 139: 23, 24; 141: 3, 4; Prov. 30: 7-9; Luke 22: 31, 32; John 17: 15.

March 9.—(Tt 5.)—Acts 14: 22; Rom. 5: 3, 4; 2 Cor.
    12: 7–10; 1 Pet. 1: 6, 7; 4: 12. 13.
March 10.—(Tt 6.)—Matt. 18: 6, 7; 1 Cor. 8: 11; Gal.
    6: 1; Heb. 3: 13.
March 11.—(Tt 7.)—Gen. 3: 1, 4, 5; Num. 22: 17;
    Josh. 7: 21; Job 1: 6-12; Mark 14: 67–72;
    John 13: 27; Acts 5: 3.

## For Meditation throughout the Week.

Do I pity myself for my temptations, as if they
were my misfortunes?  Let me rather despise
myself for my weakness, and fear for my deadly
peril.  Do I say to myself, "The next time I will
be stronger"?  I should more wisely take counsel
from the last time than from the next time, judg-
ing that where I have so often fallen I am more
likely to fall again than to amend.  Is it growing
more easy for me to resist temptations?  Nay, it
is growing more difficult; and so what warrant
have I for thinking that they will not finally
master me?  Does my hatred of sin increase, so
that I avoid it more and more?  No, alas! I strive
to get as near to it as I can without falling into it,
and when I do fall, I console myself with thinking
that it was because I misjudged and got too near;
I do not decide that I must avoid it altogether.
Oh, wretched man that I am!  Who shall deliver
me from this dead body of my sins?  Who shall
free me from this self-deception, this falseness
and emptiness and waste of life?  Thou, O Christ,
who wast tempted in all points as I am; yea, who
wast tempted as I am in this very point, to half
love sin and half to hate it.  In my own strength I
can never conquer, but in Thy strength I can
do all things; I can even gain the victory over
myself.

# The Eleventh Week.

## CONSCIENCE.

### (Symbol, Cn.)

## Sub-Topics and Leading Texts.

March 12.—*Conscience is from God.*  Prov. 20: 27. (Cn 1.)

March 13.—*The authority of conscience.*  1 Tim. 1: 19.  (Cn 2.)

March 14. -- *Varying consciences.*  Rom. 14: 14–23. (Cn 3.)

March 15.—*Evil consciences.*  Prov. 28: 1.  (Cn 4.)

March 16.—*Good consciences.*  1 John 3: 21, 22, (Cn 5.)

March 17.—*Consciences aroused; Old Testament.* Job 42: 5, 6.  (Cn 6.)

March 18.—*Consciences aroused; New Testament.* Luke 22: 61, 62.  (Cn 7.)

## Texts to be Linked with the Principal Ones.

March 12.—(Cn 1.)—Isa. 6: 5; Rom. 2: 14–16.

March 13.—(Cn 2.)—Rom. 13: 5; 1 Tim. 3: 9; 1 Pet. 2: 19.

March 14.—(Cn 3.)—1 Cor. 8: 7–13; 10: 25–33.

March 15.—(Cn 4.)—Acts 26: 9–11; 1 Tim. 4: 2; Tit. 1: 15; Heb. 9: 13, 14; 10: 22; Rev. 6: 15–17.

March 16.—(Cn 5.)—Prov. 5: 1, 11–14; Acts 23: 1; 24: 16; Heb. 13: 18.

March 17.—(Cn 6.)—Gen. 4: 13: 42: 21; Lev. 26: 36; Deut. 28: 34, 65–67; 2 Sam. 24: 10; Ps. 38: 1–6; Ezek. 7: 16–18, 25, 26; Dan. 5: 5, 6.

March 18.—(Cn 7.)—Matt. 24:30; 27:3–5; Luke 5: 8; John 8:7–9; Acts 2:37; 16:29; 24:25.

## For Meditation throughout the Week.

What a wonderful force is this that I carry within myself, a force that exercises authority over myself; that bends me as it will, either to evil or to good; that makes me or ruins me, and at the same time makes or ruins itself; and will live with me, foul or ennobled, through ages of ages! And how little time I spend in instructing this conscience of mine; how heedlessly I permit it to go its way, and lead me with it, to doom or bliss! Sometimes it speaks with the voice of God; sometimes I allow the Adversary to use it for his evil mouthpiece. Oh, purify my conscience, Thou God of all spirits; purify it from dead works to serve Thee unto life eternal. May all things pure and good be my meditation; may all holy ambitions be my only desire; give me power to throttle base passions at their birth. Let shameful words die upon my lips unsaid, and base thoughts die within my heart uncherished. Make it as easy for me to do right as it now is easy to do wrong. Dwell Thou in me, and permit me to dwell in Thee, that Thy conscience may be my conscience, and Thy thoughts my thoughts, forever and ever. Amen.

# The Twelfth Week.

## REPENTANCE.

### (Symbol, R.)

## Sub-Topics and Leading Texts.

March 19.—*A time for repentance.* Isa. 55:6, 7
(R 1.)

March 20.—*Summons to repent.* Isa. 1:16, 17.
(R 2.)

March 21.—*God inspires repentance.* Ezek. 11:
19, 20. (R 3.)

March 22.—*God's response to repentance.* Ps. 34:
14, 18. (R 4.)

March 23.—*Seeking and finding.* Deut. 4:29.
(R 5.)

March 24.—*Confidence in repentance.* Ezek. 18:
21–23. (R 6.)

March 25.—*Prove repentance by deeds.* Matt. 3:
7, 8. (R 7.)

## Texts to be Linked with the Principal Ones.

March 19.—(R 1.)—Ps. 95:7, 8; Hos. 10:12; 12:6;
Matt. 4:17; Mark 1:4, 15.

March 20.—(R 2.)—Deut. 32:29; Prov. 1:22, 23;
Jer. 13:15, 16; Joel 2:12, 13; Amos 4:12;
5:14, 15; Mark 2:17; Luke 13:3; Rev. 2:
5, 16.

March 21.—(R 3.)—Job 36:10; Isa. 57:15; 66:1, 2;
Jer. 3:12–14; 4:1, 3, 14; 6:8, 16; 24:7;
Zech. 12:10–12; Acts 5:31; Rom. 2:4;
2 Tim. 2:25.

March 22.—(R 4.)—Deut. 30:2, 3; 2 Chron. 7:14;
Neh. 1:9; Ps. 51:17; 147:3; Isa. 61:1, 2;
Luke 15:7.

March 23.—(R 5.)—2 Chron. 30 : 9; Zech. 1 : 3; Luke 18 : 13, 14; Jas. 4 : 8-10.

March 24.—(R 6.)—Isa. 44 : 22; 59 : 20; Ezek. 33 : 10-12.

March 25.—(R 7.)—1 Sam. 7 : 3; Job 11 : 13-19; 22 : 23; Acts 26 : 20; Heb. 6 : 1.

## For Meditation throughout the Week.

Oh, the goodness of God that leadeth me to repentance! That bears with me so tenderly day after day, enduring my sins so patiently, striving with my waywardness so faithfully, encouraging my faint reforms, and constantly ministering to me all the pure incentives of the natural and the spiritual world! Ungrateful wretch that I am, not long ago to turn decisively from the sins that make Him mourn, not long ago to accept with eagerness the pardon so freely offered, not long ago to yield myself without reserve to His all-wise guidance. Lord, in my own strength I cannot repent. I am too much in love with my sins. I break away from them, and I return to them again. I hate them, and still they fascinate me. When my thoughts would be upon Thee, they are upon them. My will is theirs, and not Thine. But Thou canst make it Thine. Repentance is Thy gift, O God, if I will but ask for it in faith. And I do ask for it. I do trust in Thee, not only to cleanse me from sin, not only to turn me toward Thyself, but to make me desire purification, desire to turn. Thou didst come to call sinners to repentance, and Thou art still bestowing the spirit of repentance upon men. Bestow that spirit upon me, I pray Thee with all my soul. Amen.

# The Thirteenth Week.

## CONVERSION.

(Symbol, Λ, an inverted V.)

### Sub-Topics and Leading Texts.

March 26.—*Conversion necessary.* John 3:3, 5. (Λ 1.)

March 27.—*The source of conversions.* John 6: 44. (Λ 2.)

March 28.—*Regeneration.* 2 Cor. 5:17. (Λ 3.)

March 29.—*The duty of converting others.* Matt. 5:13-16. (Λ 4.)

March 30.—*The reward of converting others.* Dan. 12:3. (Λ 5.)

March 31.—*How to win others: Old Testament.* Num. 10:29. (Λ 6.)

April 1.—*How to win others: New Testament.* Acts 4:13, 20. (Λ 7.)

### Texts to be Linked with the Principal Ones.

March 26.—(Λ 1.)—Jer. 44:5, 11; Ezek. 3:19; Matt. 18:3.

March 27.—(Λ 2.)—1 Kings 8:57, 58; 18:37; Ps. 36: 9; Prov. 1:23; Isa. 44:3-5; Jer. 24:7; Hos. 11:4; Acts 3:26; 26:18.

March 28.—(Λ 3.)—Jer. 3:17; Matt. 13:33; Luke 22:32; John 1:16; 4:14; Rom. 6:18; 12: 2; Eph. 4:21-24.

March 29.—(Λ 4.)—Ps. 60:4; 96:3; Prov. 11:30; Isa. 43:12; 62:6; Phil. 2:15, 16; Col. 4:5; Jude 3, 22, 23.

March 30.—(Λ 5.)—Jas. 5:19, 20.

March 31.—(Λ 6.)—1 Kings 22:14; Ps. 40:9, 10; 51: 6-13; 67:1, 2; Mic. 3:8.

April 1.—(Λ 7.)—Mark 5:20; 16:20; Acts 5:42; 6: 4, 10; 8:35; 2 Cor. 8:5.

## For Meditation throughout the Week.

The new life! How blessed to turn from the sins of which I am so weary, the temptations against which I have struggled so long in vain, the failures and punishments of the past, to a life of triumph, of purity, and peace! For every pleasure I leave behind, I have found ten thousand joys; for every ambition discarded, I have reached ten thousand nobler glories; for every promise of Satan's, I have a myriad of God's fulfilments. What a change in the prospect, now I have turned! Then downhill, now ever upward to the city of gold; then into ever growing darkness, now into constantly increasing light; then amid thorns and poisonous exhalations, now where all flowers scent the air. And how can I praise God, who has called me to Himself? How, but by calling others to come along with me? O my Saviour, who hast had mercy upon me, give boldness to my tongue and constancy to my heart. May it be through no fault of mine that others still wander in the darkness from which I am free. Thou hast saved me, O Christ; help me to save some one else. Amen.

# The Fourteenth Week.

## CONFESSION.

### (Symbol, Cf.)

### Sub-Topics and Leading Texts.

April 2.—*Confession required.* Num. 5:6, 7. (Cf 1.)

April 3.—*Confession regarded.* 1 John 1:9. (Cf 2.)

April 4.—*Promises to confession.* Prov. 28:13. (Cf 3.)

April 5.—*Humility in confession.* Luke 15:18, 19. (Cf 4.)

April 6.—*A full confession.* Ps. 32:5. (Cf 5.)

April 7.—*Confession before God and men.* Ps. 51: 3, 4. (Cf 6.)

April 8.—*Examples of good confession.* Acts 19: 18, 19. (Cf 7.)

### Texts to be Linked with the Principal Ones.

April 2.—(Cf 1.)—Lev. 5:5; 16:21; Josh. 7:19; Ezra 10:11; Jer. 3:13.

April 3.—(Cf 2.)—Ezek. 33:10–12; Hos. 5:15.

April 4.—(Cf 3.)—Lev. 26:40–42.

April 5.—(Cf 4.)—Ezra 9:6; Job 13:23; Isa. 6:5; 64:6; 1 Cor. 15:9; 2 Cor. 7:9–11.

April 6.—(Cf 5.)—Neh. 1:6, 7; Lam. 3:40–42.

April 7.—(Cf 6.)—Ps. 38:18; Hos. 14:1, 2; Jonah 3: 8, 9; Rom. 14:11; Jas. 5:16.

April 8.—(Cf 7.)—Gen. 42:21; Num. 12:11; 22:
    31, 34; 1 Sam. 15:24; 2 Sam. 12:13; 24:10;
    1 Kings 21:27-29; 2 Chron. 32:26; 33:
    12, 13.

## For Meditation throughout the Week.

What confession does God require me to make of my sins? I am willing to confess them before Him. Nay, I do confess them day and night with fear and shame. But I am not willing to confess them before men. How much I must think of men, and how little of God! Had I the conception I should have of men's iniquity and God's purity, of men's weakness and God's infinite power, of the worthlessness of most human praise and the eternal worth of God's approval, it would be different: I should freely confess my sins before men, but I should enter with trembling and shrinking of soul into the presence of a justly offended God. Wherever I have sinned, O God, and wherever my confession may draw others from sin, and even wherever my confession may strengthen me in my good purposes, grant me the power to make it, though all men hiss at me. Give me a clear view of my sin. Show me my heart just as it is. Let me not cheat myself by any evasion or compromise. And lead me, by paths of openness and honesty and humility, closer, O God, to Thee. Amen.

# The Fifteenth Week.

## SALVATION.

### (Symbol, S.)

### Sub-Topics and Leading Texts.

April 9.—*Christ's own words promising salvation.* Luke 19:10. (S 1.)

April 10.—*From what Christ saves.* Eph. 2:1–17. (S 2.)

April 11.—*Whom Christ saves.* Acts 2:39. (S 3.)

April 12.—*What salvation accomplishes.* John 3:16, 17. (S 4.)

April 13.—*Parables of salvation.* John 10:1-7. (S 5.)

April 14.—*Salvation rejected.* John 5:40. (S 6.)

April 15.—*Salvation accepted.* 1 Cor. 6:11. (S 7.)

### Texts to be Linked with the Principal Ones.

April 9.—(S 1.)—Mark 2:17; John 7:37.

April 10.—(S 2.)—Matt. 11:28–30; Gal. 3:13; Rev. 3:17–20.

April 11.—(S 3.)—John 6:37; Acts 10:34, 35; 13:26, 47; Rom. 1:16; 10:13; 1 Tim. 2:3–6; 4:10; Rev. 5:9; 7:9.

April 12.—(S 4.)—Luke 2:10, 31, 32; John 4:14; Rom. 10:11; Eph. 5:14.

April 13.—(S 5.)—Luke 14:16–24; 15:4-10, 11–32; 16:19–31; John 15:1–5.

April 14.—(S 6.)—Matt. 21: 31; 23: 37.
April 15.—(S 7.)—1 Tim. 1: 15; Titus 3: 3–5.

## For Meditation Throughout the Week.

I do not need to be trained, I need to be re-formed. I do not need to be helped, I need to be redeemed. I do not need to be encouraged, I need to be saved. I do not foolishly believe that only a small thing is wrong with me, I know that all is wrong with me. The disease of sin has infested every part, the blindness of sin has utterly put out my eyes, the death which is sin has control of the castle of life, and unless Christ saves me, I am all undone. But Christ *will* save me, Christ *has* saved me! Oh, the joy, the triumph of the thought! Now I can sing with all angels, and work with all men. Now I can look up to heaven, I, who before could not even through shame look into the face of men, or into my own heart. It was a royal gift, undeserved, unearned, unrequited. It was a gift such as God alone could bestow and Christ alone could bring. All eternity will not suffice to praise Him. All my time and energies will pay no fraction of the debt. Yet I will give them because they are His, and because I love Him, and because of His great love to me.

# The Sixteenth Week.

## WATCHFULNESS.

### (Symbol, Wt.)

### Sub-Topics and Leading Texts.

April 16.—*Watch your heart.* Prov. 4:23. (Wt 1.)

April 17.—*How to watch.* Eph. 6:18. (Wt 2.)

April 18.—*Watch against worldliness.* Ex. 34:12. (Wt 3.)

April 19.—*Watch against unfaithfulness.* Deut. 4:9, 23. (Wt 4.)

April 20.—*Watch against sin.* Mark 14:38. (Wt 5.)

April 21.—*Watch for chances to do good.* Josh. 22:5. (Wt 6.)

April 22.—*The reward of watchfulness.* Luke 21: 36. (Wt 7.)

### Texts to be Linked with the Principal Ones.

April 16.—(Wt 1.)—Josh. 23:11; Prov. 28:26; 1 Cor. 10:12; Heb. 3:12.

April 17.—(Wt 2.)—Ps. 4:4; 119:9; Prov. 4:25, 26; Eph. 5:15; 1 Thess. 5:4, 6; 2 Tim. 4:5; 1 Pet. 4:7.

April 18.—(Wt 3.)—Luke 11:35; 12:15; 2 Pet. 3:17.

April 19.—(Wt 4.)—Matt. 25:13; Luke 12:35-40; Heb. 2:1; Rev. 3:2, 3.

April 20.—(Wt 5.)—Deut. 11:16; Job 36:21; 1 Pet. 5:8.

April 21.—(Wt 6.)—1 Cor. 16:13; 2 Tim. 1:6; Heb. 6:11, 12.

April 22.—(Wt 7.)—1 Kings 2:4; 1 John 5:18; 2 John 8; Rev. 16:15.

## For Meditation throughout the Week.

How can I watch against the sins that beset me? In the first place by learning to hate them. No sentry will be faithful, under whatever penalties, if he loves the foe. Let me learn to see and know the ugliness of sin. In the second place, by learning to love God. No watch so faithful as a lover's, and when God has become the sum of my desires, I shall need no prompting to watchfulness in His service. And in the third place, let me understand myself, let me be honest with my conscience, let me acknowledge my faults before God and man. An enemy is half conquered that is wholly recognized. O Thou whose watchful eye is ever upon me; Thou who dost never sleep, in order that Thy children may enjoy the delights of slumber,—can I not watch with Thee one hour? I will guard jealously this trust Thou hast committed to me. I will not make myself an ally of the foe. And I know that if my heart is right with Thee, Thou wilt not let my eyelids close on guard, and Thou wilt keep my body upright.

# The Seventeenth Week.

## DEATH.

### (Symbol, D.)

### Sub-Topics and Leading Texts.

April 23.—*What death is.*  Ps. 103: 14–16.  (D 1.)

April 24.—*The fear of death.*  Matt. 10: 28.  (D 2.)

April 25.—*The conquest of death.*  1 Cor. 15: 12–58.
(D 3.)

April 26.—*Readiness for death.*  Ps. 90: 12.  (D 4.)

April 27.—*Spiritual death.*  Rom. 8: 5–8, 13.  (D 5.)

April 28.—*How the wicked die.*  Ps. 92: 7.  (D 6.)

April 29.—*How the good die.*  Ps. 23: 4.  (D 7.)

### Texts to be Linked with the Principal Ones.

April 23.—(D 1.)—Gen. 3: 19; Josh. 23: 14; 1 Sam.
2: 6; 2 Sam. 14: 14; Job 7: 10; 14: 1, 2;
Eccl. 8: 8; 12: 1–7; Isa. 40: 6, 7; John 11:
11–14; 1 Tim. 6: 7; Heb. 9: 27; 13: 14; Jas.
1: 10, 11.

April 24.—(D 2.)—2 Sam. 12: 23; Job 3: 13–22; Eccl.
7: 2; Rom. 14: 8, 9.

April 25.—(D 3.)—Job 14: 14; 1 Cor. 3: 22; Phil. 1:
20–23; Heb. 2: 14, 15; Rev. 20: 14.

April 26.—(D 4.)—Deut. 32: 29; 1 Sam. 20: 3; 2
Kings 20: 1; Job 7: 1; Ps. 39: 4; Eccl. 9:
10; 11: 7, 8; Isa. 38: 18, 19; Luke 12: 37;
John 9: 4; Jas. 4: 15.

April 27.—(D 5.)—Isa. 1: 5; 64: 6; Luke 1: 79; Acts
8: 23; Rom. 5: 12: Eph. 2: 1; 5: 14; Col. 2:
13.

April 28.—(D 6.)—2 Chron. 21:20; Job 18:14–18; 24:19-24; Ps. 37:1, 2, 9, 10, 35, 36; 49:20; 55:23; Prov. 2:22; 13:9; 29:1; 1 Thess. 5:3.

April 29.—(D 7.)—Gen. 15:15; Num. 23:10; Ps. 37:37; 49:15; 116:15; Prov. 14:32; Luke 2:29; Acts 7:59; 2 Cor. 5:1–8; 1 Thess. 4:13, 14; 2 Tim. 4:6–8; Heb. 11:13; Rev. 14:13.

## For Meditation throughout the Week.

Oh, solemn and momentous event, mysterious, dread, and inevitable! Oh, joyous and fortunate event, the opening of prison, the portal of paradise! If I should spend my days and nights in fear of it, I should do wisely. If I should pass my time in longing for it, I should do even more wisely. My sins alone render its approach terrible, and there is One standing by my side who has become sin for me, who has confronted death for me, who has placed in my hand a warrant of immunity from all Death's just attacks, sealed with His victorious blood. He has conquered for me the last enemy. What then have I but a welcoming hand for thee, O escort Death! Thou shalt show me the way out of all my perplexities and pains and tears, out of all my temptations and bitter memories and harassing doubts, and thou wilt lead me into the eternal sunshine. I will not dread thy approach, for myself or my dear ones. For them, as for me, that approach is the end of sorrows and of partial joys, and the beginning of perfect happiness. Only do Thou go with me, my Saviour, for I dare not walk with Death alone.

# The Eighteenth Week.

## JUDGMENT.

### (Symbol, J.)

### Sub-Topics and Leading Texts.

April 30.—*The time of the Judgment.* Mark 13: 28–37. (J 1.)

May 1.—*Who are to be judged.* Rom. 14: 10–12. (J 2.)

May 2.—*How they will be judged.* Matt. 25: 31–33. (J 3.)

May 3.—*The rewards of the Judgment.* Matt. 16: 27. (J 4.)

May 4.—*The penalties of the Judgment.* Matt. 7: 22, 23. (J 5.)

May 5.—*Safety in the Judgment.* Jude 24, 25. (J 6.)

May 6.—*The expectation of the Judgment.* Eccl. 11: 9. (J 7.)

### Texts to be Linked with the Principal Ones.

April 30.—(J 1.)—Prov. 11: 31; Acts 17: 31; 1 Cor. 4: 5; 1 Pet. 4: 7.

May 1.—(J 2.)—Eccl. 3: 17; 12: 14; Rom. 2: 5–12; 1 Cor. 3: 8, 13–15; 1 Pet. 1: 17.

May 2.—(J 3.)—Job 34: 11; Isa. 34: 4; 51: 6; Ezek. 33: 20; Dan. 7: 9, 10; Matt. 12: 37; 24: 29–35; Luke 12: 47, 48; John 12: 48; Jas. 2: 12, 13; Jude 6–15; Rev. 1: 7; 2: 23; 20: 11–15; 22: 12.

44

May 3.—(J 4.)—Prov. 12:14; Matt. 13:43; 1 Cor. 6:
2, 3; 2 Tim. 4:1, 8.

May 4.—(J 5.)—Job 21:30; Jer. 17:10; Ezek. 7:3,
27; 18:20; Matt. 10:14, 15; 11:22; 12:36;
13:30, 40–42; 22:13; 2 Thess. 1:7, 8; 2 Pet.
2:9.

May 5.—(J 6.)—Gen. 4:7; Prov. 24:12; Isa. 3:10;
Joel 3:15, 16; 1 John 4:17.

May 6.—(J 7.)—Luke 12:2; Acts 24:25; 2 Cor. 5:
10; Heb. 2:2, 3; 10:27; 12:25; 2 Pet. 3:
7–12.

### For Meditation throughout the Week.

How shall I be able to stand before the Judge, I
with my ungrateful heart, my discontent, my
murmurings against Providence, my cowardice in
the presence of evil, my sluggishness in the
service of good, my secret sins, my open sins, my
unkind words, my shameful thoughts? What de-
spair will fill me when I come to stand before the
Pure One, whose justice burns as a furnace,
whose anger can annihilate a world! Nay, I shall
stand there with perfect calmness and confidence.
Yes, remembering all my sins, not forgetting one
of the black catalogue, yet I shall stand there
without trembling. For Thou wilt stand by my
side, O my Advocate! Thou wilt show the nail-
prints in Thy hands, the bleeding wound in Thy
side. Thou wilt plead Bethlehem, Thou wilt
plead Calvary. For Thou art the Mercy of God,
Compassionate One, and I trust in Thee. When
I come to stand before the Justice of God, I shall
have no other trust. Thou art my confidence now,
and Thou wilt not fail me then. Through all the
judgments of the present Thou art conducting
me, as daily I struggle against temptation, fall
beneath it, and rise again. Every day of my life
Thou art showing me what Thou wilt do when the
great day comes. I shall praise Thee for this,
world without end. Amen.

# The Nineteenth Week.

## HEAVEN.

### (Symbol, H.)

## Sub-Topics and Leading Texts.

May 7.—*Getting to heaven.* Heb. 13:14. ( H1.)

May 8.—*The population of heaven.* Heb. 12:22-24. (H 2.)

May 0.—*Shut out from heaven.* Matt. 25:41-46. (H 3.)

May 10.—*Pictures of heaven.* Rev. 21:1-5, 11-27; 22:1-5. (H 4.)

May 11.—*The joys of heaven.* Ps. 16:11. (H 5.)

May 12.—*Occupation in heaven.* Rev. 7:9-17. (H 6.)

May 13.—*Glimpses of heaven.* Isa. 33:17. (H 7.)

## Texts to be Linked with the Principal Ones.

May 7.—(H 1.)—Ps. 73:24; Matt. 6:20; Luke 16:22; John 13:36.

May 8.—(H 2.)—1 Kings 8:27, 30; 22:19; Dan. 12:3; Mal. 3:17; Matt. 8:11; Luke 10:20; John 5:29.

May 9.—(H 3.)—Matt. 13:30, 41, 42, 49; Mark 9:43, 44; Luke 16:23-26; 1 Cor. 6:9, 10; 2 Thess. 1:8, 9; Rev. 21:8, 27.

May 10.—(H 4.)—Ps. 11:4; John 14:2, 3; 1 Cor. 2:9; 2 Cor. 5:1; Heb. 11:10, 16.

May 11.—(H 5.)—1 Chron. 16:27; Ps. 17:15; Isa. 25:8; 51:11; Matt. 5:8, 12; 25:34; Luke 15:7; 1 Pet. 1:4.

May 12.—(H 6.)—Matt. 18:10; 22:30; Luke 22:30; Heb. 4:9; 1 John 3:2; Rev. 2:7, 17; 3:4, 12, 21; 5:9.

May 13.—(H 7.)—Luke 2:13, 14; 20:36; 23:43; Acts 7:55; 1 Cor. 15:50; 2 Cor. 12:4; 2 Pet. 3:13.

## For Meditation throughout the Week.

Heaven must be a happy place indeed, with no pain, no sorrow, no death, and no sin; but let me not think so much of what is not in heaven as of what is there, the spirits of the just made perfect, the blessed Christ of Calvary, the Holy Spirit of all truth, the omnipotent, omniscient, all-loving Father! And let me not, either, think so much of going to heaven myself as of getting others there. Let me meditate upon the woes of those that are without. Let my heart bleed for them, as Christ's did. In nothing is their condition so sad as in this, that they do not know how sad it is. Could even heaven be a happy place for me if any of these were rejected through fault of mine? if a word I was too cowardly or careless to utter might have saved some soul? Nay, if my life on earth is thus recreant, what right shall I have to an entrance into heaven? Quicken me with Thy Spirit, O Thou who didst come from heaven to earth, so that, by a noble life on earth, I may fit myself for heaven. Amen.

# The Twentieth Week.

## IMMORTALITY.

### (Symbol, I.)

### Sub-Topics and Leading Texts.

May 14.—*Safe with God.* Ps. 121:8. (I 1.)

May 15.—*Immortality a gift.* Rom. 6:23. (I 2.)

May 16.—*Whose is eternal life?* John 12:25. (I 3.)

May 17.—*The value of immortality.* Matt. 16:26. (I 4.)

May 18.—*Evidences of immortality.* 2 Tim. 1:10. (I 5.)

May 19.—*Comfort in immortality.* Isa. 25:8. (I 6.)

May 20.—*Courage from immortality.* Matt. 10:28. (I 7.)

### Texts to be Linked with the Principal Ones.

May 14.—(I 1.)—Gen. 5:24.

May 15.—(I 2.)—Ps. 21:4; Eccl. 12:7; 1 John 2:25.

May 16.—(I 3.)—Matt. 19:29; John 10:27-29; Gal. 6:8; Tit. 3:7; 1 John 5:13.

May 17.—(I 4.)—Eccl. 3:21; 1 Tim. 4:8.

May 18.—(I 5.)—2 Kings 2:11; Matt. 17:2, 3; John 11:44; Heb. 11:5.

May 19.—(I 6.)—2 Sam. 12:23; Luke 20:36.

May 20.—(I 7.)—1 Cor. 15:53-57; Tit. 1:2.

### For Meditation throughout the Week.

Thou mightest have made me, gracious Father, the creature of a beautiful day, swallowed up and entirely lost in the night of death. But then Thou couldst not have given me these longings for eternal life, these desires the world can never satisfy, this spirit that beats against the bars of its prison house and is ever trying its wings for flight. The level of the ox would have held me then. I should have had no need of Christ and His resurrection. Nay, the word of such a thing would have been meaningless to me. But Thou hadst higher purposes in my creation, O Most High! How can I praise Thee for it? Thou wouldst make me like Thyself. Thou wouldst fashion me in the image of Thine endless years. Lord, I will wrap me in the royal robe of my immortality. I will mount this throne of boundless time. I will live more worthily of its dignity. Whatever losses may come, I shall not lose this; whatever disappointments may come, of this I shall not fail. Only to be worthy of it! Let me die with Thee, O Christ, that I may rise into Thine own eternal life!

# The Twenty=first Week.

## COMMUNION.

### (Symbol, Cm.)

### Sub-Topics and Leading Texts.

May 21.—*Origin of the Lord's Supper.* 1 Cor. 11: 23–26. (Cm 1.)

May 22.—*Right use of the Lord's Supper.* 1 Cor. 11: 27–34. (Cm 2.)

May 23.—*" The communion of saints."* 1 John 1: 7. (Cm 3.)

May 24.—*Brothers in Christ.* Eph. 4: 32. (Cm 4.)

May 25.—*Communion with God.* 1 John 1: 3. (Cm 5.)

May 26.—*How to get close to God.* John 14: 23. (Cm 6.)

May 27.—*The joy of communion.* Ps. 16: 7–9. (Cm 7.)

### Texts to be Linked with the Principal Ones.

May 21.—(Cm 1.)—Ex. 12: 21–28; Matt. 26: 26–28; Luke 22: 17–20; Acts 2: 42; 20: 7.

May 22.—(Cm 2.)—1 Cor. 10: 16–21; 5: 7, 8.

May 23.—(Cm 3.)—1 Sam. 23: 16; Ps. 55: 14; 119: 63; Gal. 2: 9; Eph. 5: 11.

May 24.—(Cm 4.)—Rom. 12: 15; Eph. 6: 18; Col. 3: 16; 1 Thess. 4: 18; 5: 11.

May 25.—(Cm 5.)—Amos 3: 3; Luke 24: 32; 1 Cor. 1: 9; 2 Cor. 6: 16; 13: 14; Phil. 2: 1; Rev. 3: 20.

May 26.—(Cm 6.)—Ps. 42:1; 63:5, 6; Phil. 1:23; 4. 6; Heb. 4:16.

May 27.—(Cm 7.)—Ps. 42:4; 133:1-3; Rom. 15:32.

## For Meditation throughout the Week.

What overflowing provision hast Thou made against my loneliness, my Father! Wherever I go I find the world full of good men who are seeking the noblest things, men who know Thee, men who hail me as a brother. Wherever I go I find Thee, my Father, my Elder Brother, my Comforter. The day is eloquent with Thee, and the night is light about me with the glow of Thy presence. When I speak, Thou dost answer; and when I listen, Thou art calling to me. Upon every hilltop I see the shining of Thy throne. In every valley is a temple where Thou dost dwell. Where a single brother of mine meets with me, Thou art in the midst of us. How can I forget these clouds of witnesses? How can I faint, with all these co-workers? How can I for a moment stoop to shamefulness when Thou art by my side? It is because I have so little mind to my communion with Thy saints and with Thee. It is because I am so earthly and Thou art heavenly. But Thou wilt ransom me even out of this, and Thou, O God, wilt make communion my chief delight, and wilt fit me for the communion that never ends.

# The Twenty=second Week.

## PROVIDENCE.

(Symbol, Pv.)

### Sub-Topics and Leading Texts.

May 28.—*God's providence mysterious.* Ps. 73: 1-17. (Pv 1.)

May 29.—*God's providence omnipotent.* Ps. 76:10. (Pv 2.)

May 30.—*God's providence conditioned.* Deut. 5:29. (Pv 3.)

May 31.—*God's providence kind.* Rom. 8:28. (Pv 4).

June 1.—*God's providence far-seeing.* Matt. 25: 34. (Pv 5.)

June 2.—*God's providence compensating.* Job 5: 12, 13. (Pv 6.)

June 3.—*God's providence just.* Ps. 111:5. (Pv 7.)

### Texts to be Linked with the Principal Ones.

May 28.—(Pv 1.)—Job 33: 12, 13; Ps. 10: 5; Eccl. 9: 2, 11; Jer. 12: 1, 2; Acts 1: 7.

May 29.—(Pv 2.)—Ex. 33: 19; Ps. 75: 7; Prov. 16: 33; 19: 21; Jer. 51: 20, 21.

May 30.—(Pv 3.)—Ex. 23: 22; Josh 1: 8; 1 Chron. 28: 8; Job 36: 11; Ps. 37: 4, 34; Prov. 2: 21; Isa. 1: 19; Zech. 3: 7; Mal. 3: 10-12.

May 31.—(Pv 4.)—Lev. 26: 1-13; Deut. 23: 5; Ps. 33: 12; 65: 4; Isa. 54: 17.

June 1.—(Pv 5.)—Ex. 9: 16; Acts 2: 23; 3: 18; 17: 26; Rom. 8: 29, 30; Eph. 1: 4-11; 3: 11.

June 2.—(Pv 6.)—Gen. 50:20; Esth. 7:10; Prov. 28:8; Eccl. 2:26; Ezek. 21:26, 27; Phil. 1: 12; Philem. 15.

June 3.—(Pv 7.)—Prov. 13:22; 14:19; 16:7; Isa. 45:5, 13; Luke 22:22.

## For Meditation throughout the Week.

I praise Thee, O God, who hast made room in all Thy boundless majesty, which owns all things, and every thought is a law—that Thou hast made room, nevertheless, for my free will. How Thou canst thrust me out from the circle of Thine omnipotence, so that I can even oppose my desires to Thy desires, and my determination to Thine age-long purposes, I know not, nor can I hope to know. I only know that Thou hast given me this wonderful power. And I bless Thee even more for this, that, having pushed me forth from the nest and bade me use my wings, Thy providence still follows lovingly, still broods above me, still allows me to take refuge beneath its feathers. It is such a comfort to know that Thou art planning for me! That when I blunder Thou art devising a remedy, that when I sin Thou hast prepared the sacrifice. With all the powers Thou hast given me, I yield myself to Thee and to Thy perfect providence. Amen.

# The Twenty=third Week.

## FAITH.

### (Symbol, F.)

### Sub-Topics and Leading Texts.

June 4.—*What it is.*  Heb. 11:1.  (F 1.)

June 5.—*What it does.*  Isa. 26:3.  (F 2.)

June 6.—*How to get it.*  1 Cor. 2:5.  (F 3.)

June 7.—*How to lose it.*  1 Tim. 1:19.  (F 4.)

June 8.—*What to do with it.*  1 John 5:4.  (F 5.)

June 9.—*Examples of faith.*  Heb. 11:2-40.  (F 6.)

June 10.—*Faith in Christ.*  Eph. 3:17.  (F 7.)

### Texts to be Linked with the Principal Ones.

June 4.—(F 1.)—Ps. 115:9;  Prov. 3:5, 6;  18:10;
Isa. 41:10, 13;  Eph. 6:16;  1 Thess. 5:8;
1 Pet. 5:7.

June 5.—(F 2.)—Deut. 31:8;  Josh. 1:9;  Ps. 5:11;
18:30, 31;  32:10;  55:22;  125:1, 2;  Prov.
16:20;  30:5;  Isa. 43:1-5,  Jer. 17:7, 8;
Hab. 2:4.

June 6.—(F 3.)—2 Chron. 20:20;  Neh. 4:14;  Ps. 27:
14;  37:5;  91:1-16;  Prov. 16:3;  Hab. 2:3;
Luke 17:5;  Rom. 15:13;  Eph. 2:8;  1 Pet.
1:5-9, 21.

June 7.—(F 4.)—Ps. 42:5, 6;  Prov. 24:10;  Matt. 8:
26;  14:31;  Rom. 11:20;  Heb. 6:12;  1 Pet.
1:6.

June 8.—(F 5.)—2 Chron. 15:7;  Eccl. 11:1;  Zech. 8:
9;  9:12;  Matt. 6:25, 32, 33.

June 9.—(F 6.)—Gen. 15:1; Ex. 4:12; 14:13; Num. 14:8, 9; Josh. 14:12; Ruth 2:12; 1 Sam. 14:6; 2 Chron. 14:11; 32:7, 8; Neh. 2:20; Job. 13:15; Dan. 3:17; Matt. 9:22; Mark 9:23; Luke 8:50; 18:42; Acts 3:16; Gal. 3:6, 7.

June 10.—(F 7.)—Mark 9:24; 11:23, 24; John 6:29; 11:25, 26; 14:1, 11, 12; 20:27-29; Gal. 2:20; 5:6; Col. 2:7; 2 Tim. 1:12; Heb. 12:2; 1 John 3:23.

### For Meditation throughout the Week.

I believe Christ, and therefore I believe that greater things than He did, I, His disciple, may do, now that He has gone to the Father. I believe Christ, and therefore I believe that with a word I could uproot a mountain, had I faith as a grain of mustard-seed; that is, if uprooting a mountain were part of God's work for me to do. I believe that for the accomplishing of my God-given tasks all the reservoirs of divine power are open for me. I have Christ's own guaranty of that, and I trust Him. So far as I have made proof of this great privilege, I have found His words true. But, alas! why have I proved them so seldom? Why, having this glorious strength and wisdom right at hand, have I permitted my hands to hang at my side? Why, having God's resources to help me do God's work, am I not more active in my Father's business? Why? Why? Why?

# The Twenty=fourth Week.

## PEACE.

### (Symbol, Pc.)

### Sub-Topics and Leading Texts.

June 11.—*The evils of war.* Jas. 4:1-3. (Pc 1).

June 12.—*Peace among men.* Luke 2:14. (Pc 2.)

June 13.—*Peace in the soul.* Phil. 4:7, 9. (Pc 3.)

June 14.—*Peace with God.* Rom. 5:1. (Pc 4.)

June 15.—*Peacemakers.* Matt. 5:9. (Pc 5.)

June 16.—*How peace comes.* John 14:27. (Pc 6.)

June 17.—*How peace goes.* Isa. 48:18, 22. (Pc 7.)

### Texts to be Linked with the Principal Ones.

June 11.—(Pc 1.)—Ps. 68:30; Isa. 1:7; 51:19; Jer. 18:21; Lam. 5:10-15.

June 12.—(Pc 2.)—Ps. 29:11; Isa. 54:10, 13; 55:12; 65:25; 66:12.

June 13.—(Pc 3.)—Ps. 37:37; 119:165; Isa. 32:17; Luke 1:79; Rom. 8:6; Col. 3:15.

June 14.—(Pc 4.)—Job 34:29; Isa. 26:3, 12; Hag. 2:9; Gal. 5:22; Eph. 2:14.

June 15.—(Pc 5.)—Ps. 37:11; 120:7; Rom. 12:18; 14:19; 2 Cor. 13:11; 2 Tim. 2:22.

June 16.—(Pc 6.)—Ex. 33:14; Job 22:21; Ps. 85:8; Prov. 3:17; Isa. 27:5; Nah. 1:15; John 16:33.

June 17.—(Pc 7.)—Gen. 4:13; Ps. 31:10; Ezek. 7: 25; Luke 13:28; Rev. 9:6.

## For Meditation throughout the Week.

"There is no peace to the wicked." Ah, how well I know that! From the days when I first left the unfreighted spirit of youth behind me and found my path darkening with worries and fears, no perplexity or sorrow, no doubt or distress has assailed me that has not sprung from sin—my sin, or some one else's. That will be the peace of heaven—just to have no more sin. That would make a heaven of this earth, all the heaven man could wish or imagine,—just to have the sins of the world blotted out. What comfort! What delight in unfettered plans! What confidence for others! What buoyancy for myself! And this peace—let me never forget it—may flow in like a river upon my entranced soul at any time. I have only to abandon my sins. I have only to trust myself to the Saviour. I have only to accept the peace that He came to bring on earth. Shall I not be a peacemaker, and begin by making peace within my heart?

# The Twenty=fifth Week.

## JOY.

### (Symbol, Jy.)

### Sub-Topics and Leading Texts.

June 18.—*The source of joy.* John 15:11. (Jy 1.)

June 19.—*Joy in salvation.* Isa. 12:2, 3. (Jy 2.)

June 20.—*Joy in God.* Ps. 16:5-11. (Jy 3.)

June 21.—*Joy and duty.* Neh. 8:10. (Jy 4.)

June 22.—*The worldling's joy.* Job 20:4, 5. (Jy 5.)

June 23.—*The Christian's joy,* John 16:22. (Jy 6.)

June 24.—*The joy eternal.* Ps. 17:15. (Jy 7.)

### Texts to be Linked with the Principal Ones.

June 18.—(Jy 1.)—Neh. 12:43; Job 8:21; Ps. 19:8; 37:4; Isa. 35:1, 2; 44:23; Jer. 15:16; Gal. 5:22; 1 Pet. 1:6-8.

June 19.—(Jy 2.)—Deut. 33:29; 1 Sam. 2:1; Ps. 13:5; 20:5; Hab. 3:17, 18.

June 20.—(Jy 3.)—1 Chron. 16:27; Ps. 5:11; 21:1, 6; 63:7; 100:1, 2; Isa. 29:19; Phil. 4:4.

June 21.—(Jy 4.)—Ps. 9:2; 27:6; 28:7; 40:16; 43:4; 126:5, 6.

June 22.—(Jy 5.)—Prov. 15:21; John 4:13.

June 23.—(Jy 6.)—Ps. 30:5, 11; 32:11; 33:21; 89:15, 16; 97:11, 12; Matt. 5:10-12; 13:44; Luke 2:10; Acts 2:46; 5:41; 13:52; 16:25, 34; 20:24; Rom. 14:17; 1 John 1:4.

June 24.—(Jy 7.)—Ps. 36:8; 46:4; 73:25, 26; Isa. 51:11; 60:20; Luke 10:20; 1 Pet. 4:13.

## For Meditation throughout the Week.

I am a free man who has shut himself up in a dungeon. I am a sound man who has chosen to use crutches. I am a man with clear vision who has bandaged his eyes. I am all of this, and more, because, when the fulness of joy has been before me ready at a grasp, ready for the asking, I have preferred the torture of my fears, the hourly harassments of my worries. And if my own gloom were all, and if I were merely lashing my own spirit with senseless thongs, it would not be so bad, but I am pouring darkness into other lives, and the folly is ever spreading; I am weakening myself for my work, and others must do what I might do if the joy of the Lord were my strength. Forgive me, blessed Master. Thou didst come to the world that Thy joy might be in us, and that our joy might be filled full. Henceforth I will not let my heart be troubled. Henceforth I will believe in Thee.

# The Twenty=sixth Week.

## HOLINESS.

### (Symbol, Hl.)

### Sub-Topics and Leading Texts.

June 25.—*Be clean.* Ps. 24:3-5. (Hl 1.)

June 26.—*Be separate.* 2 Cor. 6:16, 17. (Hl 2.)

June 27.—*Be holy.* Rom. 12:1, 2. (Hl 3.)

June 28.—*Be perfect.* 2 Cor. 7:1. (Hl 4.)

June 29.—*Depart from evil.* Ps. 37:27. (Hl 5.)

June 30.—*The way to holiness.* Eph. 2:21. (Hl 6.)

July 1.—*The rewards of holiness.* Matt. 5:8. (Hl 7.)

### Texts to be Linked with the Principal Ones.

June 25.—(Hl 1.)—Gen. 35:2; Lev. 11:44; Zech. 14:20, 21; 1 Cor. 3:16, 17; 1 Thess. 4:3, 7.

June 26.—(Hl 2.)—Deut. 14:2; Isa. 52:1, 11; John 15:19; 1 Pet. 2:9.

June 27.—(Hl 3.)—Ex. 19:6; 22:31; 39:30; Luke 1:74, 75; Rom. 6:19.

June 28.—(Hl 4.)—Gen. 17:1; Matt. 5:29, 30, 48; John 17:23; Col. 1:22.

June 29.—(Hl 5.)—Deut. 13:17; Josh. 7:12, 13; Job 28:28; Ps. 97:10; Prov. 16:17.

June 30.—(Hl 6.)—Job 36:21; Ps. 4:4; Prov. 11:23; 12:5; Isa. 35:8; Eph. 1:4; Heb. 12:1, 14, 15; 1 Pet. 1:15, 16.

July 1.—(Hl 7.)—Ps. 32:2; Rom. 6:22; 1 Tim. 4:8.

### For Meditation throughout the Week.

To be like God—that is a mighty task to set one's self. To be perfect—that is a presumptuous ideal. But the task is given me by God himself, and it is God's ideal for me. For "Ye shall be perfect" is Christ's command, and it must be possible for me. Possible to root out sin, to the last baleful germ of the poison. Possible to vanquish weakness, so that I shall move freely as the stars and resistless as the will of the Almighty. Possible to conquer worry, so that perfect peace shall fill my soul, and fill it constantly and entirely. Possible to win the zeal of Paul, the love of John, the faithfulness of Stephen. Possible to fit myself on this earth for the heaven that is only a hand's breadth away. All this is possible for me, since Christ said so—possible through His guidance and strength. O Lord Jesus, conduct me into Thy palace of delights. O my Saviour, preserve me faultless for Thy kingdom. O my Master, remove all impediments to service. And Thine shall be the praise forever. Amen.

# The Twenty=seventh Week.

## SELFISHNESS.

### (Symbol, Sl.)

### Sub-Topics and Leading Texts.

July 2.—*Self-seeking.*  Luke 6: 31-34.  (Sl 1.)

July 3.—*Self-indulgence.*  Phil. 2: 4, 20, 21.  (Sl 2.)

July 4.—*Selfish greed.*  1 Cor. 10: 24.  (Sl 3.)

July 5.—*Selfish indifference.*  Prov. 24: 11, 12.  (Sl 4.)

July 6.—*Selfish sloth.*  Num. 32: 6.  (Sl 5.)

July 7.—*Examples of selfishness.*  Luke 10: 31, 32.  (Sl 6.)

July 8.—*Examples of unselfishness.*  Gen. 13: 9.  (Sl 7.)

### Texts to be Linked with the Principal Ones.

July 2.—(Sl 1.)—Rom. 15: 1-3; Gal. 6: 2.

July 3.—(Sl 2.)—Rom. 14: 15; 2 Tim. 3: 2, 3.

July 4.—(Sl 3.)—Zech. 7: 6.

July 5.—(Sl 4.)—Ps. 38: 11; Amos 6: 6.

July 6.—(Sl 5.)—Hag. 1: 4, 9, 10; Jas. 2: 15, 16.

July 7.—(Sl 6.)—Gen. 4: 9; 13: 10, 11; Judg. 8: 6-9; 1 Sam. 30: 22; Luke 16: 19-21.

July 8.—(Sl 7.)—Gen. 14: 21-24; 23: 6, 11; 44: 33, 34; Num. 11: 29; 1 Sam. 23: 17, 18; 2 Sam. 15:

19, 20; 23:16, 17; 24:22-24; 1 Chron. 21:
17; Neh. 5:14-18; Jonah 1:12, 13; Rom.
16:3, 4; 1 Cor. 10:33; Phil. 4:17; 2 Thess.
3:8; Philem. 13, 14.

## For Meditation throughout the Week.

Selfishness is a poison, eating into all the joys
of my life. Selfishness is a sickness, wasting
away my natural strength. Selfishness is an
enemy, hating me and seeking my hurt even when
it seems to be persuading me toward the sweetest
pleasures. Selfishness is a thief, stealing from
my pocket while it feigns to put something into
my hand. How can I counteract this poison? By
the Bread of Life. Who can heal this sickness?
None but the Good Physician. What power can I
oppose to the enemy and the thief? The power
of my friend, the Captain of my salvation. Christ
cannot dwell in my heart with selfishness. O my
Master, drive the demons out, help me to cleanse
my house and garnish it, and make it Thine abode
forevermore! Then, when the spirit of love and
sacrifice has entirely filled me, then, I know, my
joy will be filled, and my peace will flow as a river
in the sunshine of Thy love.

# The Twenty=eighth Week.

## LOVE.

### (Symbol, L.)

### Sub-Topics and Leading Texts.

July 9.—*The duty and joy of love.*  1 Cor. 13:1-13.
(L 1.)

July 10.—*Love God.*  Mark 12:29, 30, 33.  (L 2.)

July 11.—*Love Christ.*  Matt. 10:37.  (L 3.)

July 12.—*Love in the home.*  Ps. 133:1.  (L 4.)

July 13.—*Love your friend.*  Prov. 17:17.  (L 5.)

July 14.—*Love your neighbor.*  Mark 12:31, 33.
(L 6.)

July 15.—*Love your enemies.* Luke 6:31-35.  (L 7.)

### Texts to be Linked with the Principal Ones.

July 9.—(L 1.)—1 Cor. 14:1; Gal. 5:6, 22; Eph. 3:
17-19; 4:15; Phil. 1:9; Jas. 1:12; 2:5;
2 Pet. 1:7; 1 John 4:17, 18; 2 John 6.

July 10.—(L 2.)—Ex. 20:6; Deut. 7:9; 10:12; 13:3;
30:6; Josh. 22:5; Ps. 31:23; 97:10; 145:
20; Prov. 8:17; Rom. 5:5; 1 Cor. 8:3.

July 11.—(L 3.)—John 8:42; 14:15, 21, 23; 15:9;
1 Cor. 16:22; 2 Cor. 5:14, 15; Eph. 6:24;
2 Thess. 3:5; 1 Pet. 1:8; 1 John 4:19.

July 12.—(L 4.)—Prov. 15:17; Song 8:6, 7.

July 13.—(L 5.)—Job 6:14; John 13:14, 15, 34, 35;
15:17; [Rom. 12:9, 10; 13:8; Eph. 5:2;
1 Pet. 4:8; 1 John 5:1-3.

July 14.—(L 6.)—Lev. 19:18, 34; Zech. 7:9; Mal.
2:10; Luke 10:36, 37; Rom. 13:9, 10; 15:
1, 2; Gal. 5:13, 14; Jas. 2:8; 1 John 3:17,
18.

July 15.—(L 7.)—Eph. 4:2, 32; 1 John 4:20.


## For Meditation throughout the Week.

If I love God perfectly, I shall receive with joy
whatever lot He sends me, and I shall praise Him
continually. I shall long for the time when I can
talk with Him, and for more leisure to read more
of His words. If I love Christ perfectly, I shall
delight to do His will, to minister to His poor and
needy, to maintain His church. I shall look forward with joyful anticipations to death, when I
shall see Him face to face. If I love men, my
brethren, I shall bear with patience all their sins,
whether they oppress me or not; I shall gladly
give up my plans when I can help them; I shall
endure without a murmur their harshness; I shall
rejoice in their welfare as much as in my own,
and seek their prosperity equally with mine.
How poor is my love, how petty, how unworthy of
Thy great love wherewith Thou hast loved me, O
my God! Take away my stony heart, and give
me a heart of flesh. Banish the spirit of hate and
the spirit of heedlessness, and fill me with the
spirit that sent Thee from heaven to earth that
there might be a Calvary and a Christ. Amen.

# The Twenty=ninth Week.

## SERVICE.

### (Symbol, Sr.)

## Sub-Topics and Leading Texts.

July 16.—*Faithful service.* Josh. 22:5. (Sr 1.)

July 17.—*Single-hearted service.* Luke 16:13. (Sr 2.)

July 18.—*Reasonable service.* Rom. 12:1. (Sr 3.)

July 19.—*Humble service.* Luke 22:26, 27. (Sr 4.)

July 20.—*Zealous service.* Col. 3:23. (Sr 5.)

July 21.—*Poor service punished.* Deut. 28:47, 48. (Sr 6.)

July 22.—*Good service rewarded.* Matt. 25:14-23. (Sr 7.)

## Texts to be Linked with the Principal Ones.

July 16.—(Sr 1.)—Ps. 40:8; John 9:4; 1 Cor. 4:2; Tit. 2:9, 10; 3:1.

July 17.—(Sr 2.)—Josh. 24:14, 22; Matt. 6:22; 1 Cor. 7:23; Eph. 6:5, 6; Col. 3:22.

July 18.—(Sr 3.)—Mal. 1:8; Luke 17:7-9.

July 19.—(Sr 4.)—1 Sam. 12:24; Ps. 123:2; Matt. 5:16; John 13:16; 1 Cor. 9:19.

July 20.—(Sr 5.)—1 Chron. 28:9; Eccl. 9:10; Eph. 6:7; 2 Tim. 1:6; Heb. 12:12.

July 21.—(Sr 6.)—Matt. 24:45-51; 25:24-30.

July 22.—(Sr 7.)—1 Kings 8: 23, 61; 2 Chron. 31: 21;
      1 Cor. 15: 58; Gal. 6: 9; Eph. 6: 8; Col. 3:
      24; Heb. 6: 11, 12; 11: 6.

## For Meditation throughout the Week.

God is serving me at all times. While I sleep, He is preparing for me rich blessings for the morrow. While I am sinning against Him, He is getting ready the joys of repentance and forgiveness, if I will only receive them. In His beautiful world He is always at work for my delight. I cannot turn anywhere without seeing the crowded evidences of His love. Best service of all, the sum of all His services, He has lived my life upon earth, He has endured my temptations, He has carried them all to the cross, He has borne them through the purifying scarlet flood, and He did it all, and does it all, with eagerness and infinite patience. What service I owe Him, what reasonable service! I will search His Word to become familiar with His will. I will do His commandments with zeal and desire. I will long for His approval, and pay no more heed to men's applause. I will not care what He sets me to do, while He works with me. I will be His bond servant, and so be mightier than any king.

# The Thirtieth Week.

## SELF-DENIAL.

### (Symbol, Sd.)

### Sub-Topics and Leading Texts.

July 23.—*What self-denial is.* Rom. 13:14. (Sd 1.)

July 24.—*What self-denial proves.* Gal. 5:24. (Sd 2.)

July 25.—*What self-denial costs.* Luke 14:26, 27, 33. (Sd 3.)

July 26.—*What self-denial gains.* Matt. 13:44-46. (Sd 4.)

July 27.—*The purpose of self-denial.* 1 Cor. 6:12. (Sd 5.)

July 28.—*Ready self-denial.* Matt. 21:3. (Sd 6.)

July 29.—*Joyous self-denial.* Acts 20:24. (Sd 7.)

### Texts to be Linked with the Principal Ones.

July 23.—(Sd 1.)—2 Sam. 24:24; Luke 21:4.

July 24.—(Sd 2.)—Gen. 22:12; Prov. 25:28.

July 25.—(Sd 3.)—Matt. 5:30; Luke 9:23, 24, 57, 58; Gal. 2:20.

July 26.—(Sd 4.)—Matt. 7:13, 14; 19:21, 27, 28; Mark 10:29, 30.

July 27.—(Sd 5.)—1 Cor. 8:9, 10, 13; 9:27.

July 28.—(Sd 6.)—Acts 21:13.

July 29.—(Sd 7.)—Phil. 3:7, 8.

### For Meditation throughout the Week.

What is this self but a gift from Christ? Shall
He that made me have no right in me? Shall it

be hard to give myself up to Him? When He asks me to forego this pleasure, that ambition, some cherished plan of mine, shall I not know that it is only to put in place of it something far better? Shall I not trust Him that made me? Whom could I trust, if not my Maker? Oh, the petty yieldings that I call self-denials, and make my boast of them as if I deserved any credit! Where is my manliness? What gratitude have I? Let me know henceforth that there is only one safety in the world, and that is Christ's will; only one palace of delight, His will; only one ambition, His approval; only one thing worth while at whatever cost, nay, though it cost all things else, —to do Christ's will. I have found the pearl of great price. It shall be no hardship to sell all that I have and buy it.

# The Thirty=first Week.

## ANGER.

### (Symbol, A.)

### Sub-Topics and Leading Texts.

July 30.—*Foolish anger.* Job. 18:4. (A 1.)

July 31.—*The evils of anger.* Job 5:2. (A 2.)

August 1.—*The cause of anger.* Gal. 5:19, 20. (A 3.)

August 2.—*The punishment of anger.* Matt. 5:22. (A 4.)

August 3.—*The cure of anger.* Eph. 4:26–31. (A 5.)

August 4.—*Righteous anger.* Mark 3:5. (A 6.)

August 5.—*God's anger.* Eph. 5:6. (A 7.)

### Texts to be Linked with the Principal Ones.

July 30.—(A 1.)—2 Chron. 28:9; Prov. 12:16; 21:24; 27:3.

July 31.—(A 2.)—Gen. 49:7; Prov. 27:4; Jas. 1:20.

August 1.—(A 3.)—Prov. 6:34; 25:28; 29:9, 22; Eccl. 7:9.

August 2.—(A 4.)—Job. 19:29; Prov. 19:19; Hos. 7:16.

August 3.—(A 5.)—Gen. 49:6; Ps. 37:8; Prov. 14:17, 29; 15:1, 18; 16:14, 32; 19:11; 29:8; Eccl. 10:4; Rom. 12:19; Col. 3:8; Jas. 1:19.

August 4.—(A 6.)—Gen. 31:36; Ex. 11:8; 32:19; Lev. 10:16; Num. 16:15; Neh. 5:6; 13:17, 25.

August 5.—(A 7.)—Gen. 6:3; 2 Kings 22:13; Job
4:9; Ps. 21:9-12; 75:8; 97:3; Isa. 30:14;
Jer. 30:23, 24; Ezek. 22:14, 20-22; Nah. 1:
2, 8–10; Hab. 3:12; Matt. 3:10; Rom. 1:
18; Rev. 19:15.

### For Meditation throughout the Week.

A parent is justly angry with a nurse if she
punishes his child, for punishment is the parent's
duty and prerogative. A teacher is wronged
when some outsider steps in to punish a scholar
for any evil deed. A government will not permit
a private citizen to kill a murderer or imprison a
thief. And shall God, the king of the universe,
shall God, the Teacher and Father of all, be
patient with me if I am angry with my brother?
Vengeance is God's, and He will recompense.
He may use me as His instrument, but let me be
very sure that I am appointed to exercise His
wrath before I strike a blow. O grant me, blessed
Jesus, Thy calmness of temper. When struck,
Thou didst not revile again. As a lamb before
her shearers is dumb, Thou openedst not Thy
mouth. Give me the courage to seem uncour-
ageous, when it is Thy will. Give me the love
that endureth all things. May I know what it is
to be crucified with Thee, and to cry even in the
supreme agony, "They know not what they do."

# The Thirty=second Week.

## FORGIVENESS.

### (Symbol, Fg.)

## Sub-Topics and Leading Texts.

August 6.—*Why to forgive.* Matt. 5:7, 45. (Fg 1.)

August 7.—*What to forgive.* Matt. 5:43–46. (Fg 2.)

August 8.—*When to forgive.* Mark 11:25. (Fg 3.)

August 9.—*How to forgive.* Rom. 12:19–21. (Fg 4.)

August 10.—*Some human examples.* Acts 7:60. (Fg 5.)

August 11.—*The Great Example.* Luke 23:34. (Fg 6.)

August 12.—*How God forgives.* Ps. 103:3–14. (Fg 7.)

## Texts to be Linked with the Principal Ones.

August 6.—(Fg 1.)—Prov. 19:11; Matt. 6:12, 14, 15; 18:32–35; Luke 6:35–37; Philem. 18.

August 7.—(Fg 2.)—Rom. 12:14, 17; Col. 3:13.

August 8.—(Fg 3.)—Prov. 24:17, 29; Luke 17:3, 4.

August 9.—(Fg 4.)—Ex. 23:4, 5; Prov. 25:21, 22; 1 Cor. 4:12, 13; Eph. 4:32; 1 Pet. 3:9.

August 10.—(Fg 5.)—Gen. 45:5–15; 50:19–21; Num. 12:1, 13; 1 Sam. 24:10–12; 2 Sam. 16:9–13; 19:19–23; 1 Kings 1:53; 2 Tim. 4:16.

August 11.—(Fg 6.)—Isa. 42:3; Matt. 9:2, 6; Luke 7:47–50; 23:42, 43; 1 Tim. 1:14, 16.

August 12.—(Fg 7.)—Gen. 8:21; 18:26; Ex. 20:6; 34:6, 7; Num. 14:18–20; 2 Sam. 24:14;

Neh. 9:17, 27–31; Ps. 85:10; 106:1; 145:8, 9; Isa. 38:17; 55:7–9; Lam. 3:22, 23, 31–33; Hos. 14:4; Luke 1:78; 6:36; 2 Cor. 1:3.

## For Meditation throughout the Week.

What am I to forgive in my brother? His harsh words, to be sure, but also his harsh thoughts. The theft he committed, to be sure, but also that he has more than I, and bears himself haughtily. I am to forgive him for what he wrongfully withholds from me, for the inadequate wages, for the lack of praise, as well as for what he actually takes from me, and for the words of undeserved blame. For the sins of omission and of commission alike I am to forgive my brother. And I am to forgive him absolutely, with no root of bitterness in my heart ready to spring up, with no reservations of judgment, nay, even with forgetfulness of the wrong I am to forgive him. And it is not to be because I am better than he, but because God is infinitely better than either of us, because my living at its best, and his living at its worst, are as one when set beside the holiness of God. Lord, I do forgive my brother, freely, fully, gladly. O forgive me, my God, for I am in sore need of Thy forgiveness. Amen.

# The Thirty=third Week.

## COVETOUSNESS.

(Symbol, Cv.)

### Sub-Topics and Leading Texts.

August 13.—*Covetousness is a sin.* Ex. 20:17. (Cv 1.)

August 14.—*The cause of covetousness.* 1 Tim. 6:5, 9-11, 17. (Cv 2.)

August 15.—*The folly of covetousness.*—Ps. 49:11-20. (Cv 3.)

August 16.—*What covetousness leads to.* Deut. 8:12-14, 17. (Cv 4.)

August 17.—*The punishment of covetousness.* Luke 6:24, 25. (Cv 5.)

August 18.—*The cure of covetousness.* Luke 12:15, 33, 34. (Cv 6.)

August 19.—*Examples of covetousness.* 1 Kings 21:1-16. (Cv 7.)

### Texts to be Linked with the Principal Ones.

August 13.—(Cv 1.)—Deut. 5:21; Ps. 10:3; Isa. 5:8; Matt. 19:24; Mark 10:24; 1 Cor. 6:10; Eph. 5:3, 5.

August 14.—(Cv 2.)—Ps. 52:7; Prov. 18:11; 28:20, 22; Isa. 55:2; Ezek. 22:12; Mark 7:21, 22.

August 15.—(Cv 3.)—Ps. 39:6; Prov. 10:2; 13:7, 11; 23:4, 5; Eccl. 4:6, 8; 5:13-17; Isa. 56:11; Hag. 1:6; Jas. 4:2, 13, 14.

August 16.— (Cv 4.)—Deut. 6: 10-12; 31: 20; Neh. 5: 7; Ps. 30: 6; Eccl. 1: 8; 5: 10-12; Ezek. 33: 31; Amos 8: 5; Mic. 2: 2; 3: 11; Hab. 1: 16; Matt. 13: 22.

August 17.—(Cv 5.)—Job 20: 15, 22, 23; 27: 16-19; Prov. 1: 19, 32; 11: 4, 24, 26, 28; 15: 6, 27; 21: 6; 22: 16; Isa. 57: 17; Jer. 17: 11; Ezek. 7: 19; Hab. 2: 6, 9, 13; Zeph. 1: 18; Jas. 1: 11; 5: 1-16.

August 18.—(Cv 6.)—Ps. 62: 10; 119: 36; Prov. 28: 16; 30: 8, 9; Matt. 6: 19, 24, 25; John 6: 27; 1 Cor. 5: 11; 7: 30, 31; Col. 3: 2, 5, 6; 1 Tim. 3: 3.

August 19.—(Cv 7.)—Gen. 3: 6; Josh. 7: 21; 1 Sam. 8: 3; 15: 8, 9; 2 Kings 5: 20-27; Matt. 19: 22; 26: 15, 16; John 6: 26; Acts 8: 18-23; 16: 19; 19: 24-27; 24: 26.

## For Meditation throughout the Week.

Covetousness! The least confessed of all sins! The least recognized to be a sin! Is it lurking in my heart? Has it crept in under the garb of ambition? In my desire to "get on in the world," am I getting glued to the world so that I can never rise above it? In my anxiety to provide for my loved ones, am I destroying my life and saddening others with miserliness? Let me consider in what spirit I bear the loss of money. Is it endured as one would endure it that had treasures in heaven? Is my heart there, or here? Let me consider how easy it is to give away my money. Is it in theory, or also in actual generous fact, that I hold all my possessions to be the Lord's? What shall I render unto the Lord for all His benefits to me? I shall count Him better than His benefits, more to be desired than any of His gifts; and while I receive with gratitude the good things He heaps upon me, I shall have gratitude enough— O grant it, my Father!—to receive above all the gifts, the blessed Giver himself.

# The Thirty-fourth Week.

## CONTENTMENT.

### (Symbol, Ct.)

## Sub-Topics and Leading Texts.

August 20.—*The duty of contentment.* Ps. 37:7. (Ct 1.)

August 21.—*The gains of contentment.* 1 Tim. 6:6. (Ct 2.)

August 22.—*The source of contentment.* Phil. 4:11, 12. (Ct 3.)

August 23.—*Reasons for contentment.* Heb. 13:5. (Ct 4.)

August 24.—*Compensations.* Prov. 15:16. (Ct 5.)

August 25.—*The golden mean.* Prov. 30:8. (Ct 6.)

August 26.—*Some contented folk.* 2 Kings 4:13. (Ct 7.)

## Texts to be Linked with the Principal Ones.

August 20.—(Ct 1.)—Luke 3:14; 1 Cor. 7:17, 20, 21; Gal. 5:26.

August 21.—(Ct 2.)—Prov. 15:13, 15, 30; 17:22; Eccl. 2:24; 3:12, 13.

August 22.—(Ct 3.)—Prov. 14:14; Eccl. 5:12.

August 23.—(Ct 4.)—Ps. 16:6; 37:16; 1 Tim. 6:7, 8.

August 24.—(Ct 5.)—Prov. 16:8; 17:1; Eccl. 4:6.

August 25.—(Ct 6.)—Eccl. 6:9.

August 26.—(Ct 7.)—Gen. 33:9; 2 Sam. 19:33–37.

### For Meditation throughout the Week.

If I am not contented with my lot, it is because I would find fault either with God, or with myself, or with other persons. If with other persons or with myself, and I can remedy the lack by greater diligence or by kindly expostulation, what folly in me to be gloomy over what is so easily bettered! And if I cannot remedy it in any such way, what folly to be discontented when nothing is to be gained by it! But, alas! most of my discontent is dissatisfaction with my Father in heaven. I would have greater abilities than He has seen fit to bestow upon me. I would find myself in an easier situation, in a more conspicuous post. I would exchange my body for a stronger one, or one more beautiful. In a thousand ways I rebel against His providence. And how foolish this is, when He is the Omnipotent One, and controls all things with a wish! And how worse than foolish it is, since He is the All-loving One, and to desire my life different from what He has planned it, is to wish it injured or utterly ruined. Lord Jesus, forgive my sinful discontent.

# The Thirty=fifth Week.

## TRUTH.

(Symbol, Tr.)

### Sub-Topics and Leading Texts.

August 27.—*Truth in heart.* Ps. 15:1-5. (Tr 1.)

August 28.—*Truth in word.* Isa. 33:15, 16. (Tr 2.)

August 29.—*Truth in action.* Prov. 4:25–27. (Tr 3.)

August 30.—*Sources of truth.* 2 Cor. 4:2. (Tr 4.)

August 31.—*Blessings of truth.* Prov. 3:3, 4. (Tr 5.)

September 1.—*Different kinds of falsehood.* Ex. 20:15, 16. (Tr 6.)

September 2.—*Punishment of falsehood.* Rev. 21: 8, 27; 22:15. (Tr 7.)

### Texts to be Linked with the Principal Ones.

August 27.—(Tr 1.)—Job 27:6; Ps. 17:3; 26:2; 51:6.

August 28.—(Tr 2.)—Prov. 20:14; Mal. 2:6; Rom. 9:1; 1 Thess. 2:4.

August 29.—(Tr 3.)—Deut. 25:13–16; Ps. 18:20; 26:1; Prov. 3:27, 28; Mic. 6:8; Heb. 13:18.

August 30.—(Tr 4.)—Deut. 16:20; Prov. 16:11; 2 Cor. 8:21; Eph. 4:25; Phil. 4:8; Col. 3:9, 22, 23.

August 31.—(Tr 5.)—Prov. 10:9; 12:22; 20:7; 28:20.

September 1.—(Tr 6.)—Ex. 23:1; Lev. 19:11, 12, 16; Ps. 12:2, 3; 55:21; 62:4; Jer. 9:3; Hos. 4:1; 12:7; Amos 8:5; Mic. 6:10, 11; Rom. 2:21; 13:8.

September 2.—(Tr 7.)—Deut. 19:18, 19; Ps. 5:6, 9;
  52:2–5; 55:23; 101:5, 7; Prov. 19:9; 20:
  17; 21:6; Nah. 3:1; Zech. 5:3, 4; 1 Thess.
  4:6.

### For Meditation throughout the Week.

In few ways am I more foolish than in cheating
myself, in persuading myself that I am better
than I am, in concealing my own motives from
myself, hiding my head in forgetfulness, and be-
lieving that thus I am hidden from God. If I can
once be honest with myself, perhaps I can be
honest with other men; but until my heart speaks
the truth, my lips and my actions will hardly be
sincere. O thou Spirit of Truth, dwell within me,
for I am sick of shams. However it may mortify
the flesh, I would know the truth about myself.
However it would shame me before men, I would
have them know the truth about me. I would
open every thought to the inspection of the universe, as it is already open to the eye of the God
of the universe. I would not live in the darkness.
I would put far from me all guile and hypocrisy.
I would speak simply, weighing my words, and
yet not needing to weigh them, for honesty should
be instinctive. Let Thy truth lead me, O God,
and let me part forever from all lies. Amen.

# The Thirty=sixth Week.

## LABOR.

### (Symbol, La.)

### Sub-Topics and Leading Texts.

September 3.—*The command to labor.* Eccl. 9:10. (La 1.)

September 4.—*The purposes of labor.* Rom. 12:11. (La 2.)

September 5.—*Diligent toil.* Eccl. 11:4, 6. (La 3.)

September 6.—*Material results of labor.* Prov. 12:11, 24, 27. (La 4.)

September 7.—*Spiritual results of labor.* Prov. 13:4. (La 5.)

September 8.—*Pictures of sloth.* Prov. 26:13–16. (La 6.)

September 9.—*The punishment of sloth.* Prov. 6:6–11. (La 7.)

### Texts to be Linked with the Principal Ones.

September 3.—(La 1.)—Gen. 2:15; Prov. 27:23; 1 Thess. 4:11; 2 Thess. 3:10, 12, 13.

September 4.—(La 2.)—Prov. 22:29; Eph. 4:28.

September 5.—(La 3.)—Prov. 20:13; 30:25, 26; 31:27.

September 6.—(La 4.)—Prov. 10:4; 13:11; 28:19.

September 7.—(La 5.)—Prov. 14:23; 21:5.

September 8.—(La 6.)—Prov. 10:5, 26; 15:19; 18:
9; 19:15; 20:4; 24:30–34; Isa. 56:10.

September 9.—(La 7.)—Prov. 12:24; 21:25; 23:21.

## For Meditation throughout the Week.

Labor is God's order for my life. In it He has concealed some of His noblest blessings for me. Through it He wishes me to accomplish much for Him and for the world. No one else can do my task, not even God Himself can do it for me. Therefore it may seem little to me, but it is great. It may seem ignoble, but the faithful performance of it is my patent of nobility. "My Father worketh hitherto," said Christ, "and I work." How ceaseless are God's labors, and how He enjoys His toil! Also it was Christ's meat and drink to be co-worker with His Father. Grant me strength, O my Master, that my determination may not falter, that my powers may not flag, that I may not be borne away from my healthful task by any of earth's glittering baubles. I would enter into Thy work, that I may enter into Thy joy. Amen.

# The Thirty=seventh Week.

## PERSEVERANCE.

### (Symbol, Pe.)

## Sub-Topics and Leading Texts.

September 10.—*Perseverance tempted.*  Eph. 4: 14. (Pe 1.)

September 11.—*Perseverance failing.*  2 John 9. (Pe 2.)

September 12.—*Holding on.*  Acts 11: 23.  (Pe 3.)

September 13.—*Upheld.*  Ps. 37: 24, 28.  (Pe 4.)

September 14.—*God's perseverance.*  Jer. 32: 40. (Pe 5.)

September 15.—*The secret of perseverance.*  Isa. 40: 31.  (Pe 6.)

September 16.—*The reward of perseverance.*  Matt. 24: 13.  (Pe 7.)

## Texts to be Linked with the Principal Ones.

September 10.—(Pe 1.)—Luke 9: 62; 22: 31, 32; John 10: 28, 29; Rom. 8: 35-39.

September 11. — (Pe 2.) — Rom. 11: 22; Heb. 2: 1; 2 Pet. 1: 10; 1 John 2: 19.

September 12.—(Pe 3.)—Deut. 11: 22; Josh. 23: 8; 1 Sam. 12: 20; Job 17: 9; Eccl. 7: 18; 1 Cor. 16: 13; Col. 1: 23; 2 Thess. 3: 13; Rev. 3: 11.

September 13.—(Pe 4.)—Ps. 73: 24; 1 Cor. 1: 8, 9; 2 Cor. 1: 21, 22; Phil. 1: 6.

September 14.—(Pe 5.)—Ps. 138: 8; Isa. 51: 6; 55: 3; 1 Thess. 5: 9, 10, 24; 2 Tim. 1: 12; Heb. 10: 23.

September 15.—(Pe 6.)—1 Chron. 16:15; Prov. 4:
    25–27; Luke 21:19; Col. 2:6, 7; 2 Thess.
    2:15–17.

September 16.—(Pe 7.)—Prov. 4:18; Hos. 6:3; John
    8:31, 32; 15:7; Rom. 2:7; 1 Cor. 15:58;
    Gal. 6:9; 2 Tim. 4:18; Heb. 3:6, 14; Rev.
    2:10, 26.

## For Meditation throughout the Week.

I give praise to the Lord that He does not give
me up! How feeble is my determination, constantly veering to this purpose and that; but His
determination never wavers, being always bent
upon my salvation. How weak is my will, that a
moment's fancy and gust of passion may turn
aside from the holiest ambition; but God's will
has made the worlds and through all ages has
preserved them, and God's will never fails His
creatures. If I trust to my own perseverance, it
breaks like a straw beneath me. I may trust in
God's perseverance. He will watch over me when
my eyes are closed. He will ward off the enemies
that creep up behind my back. He will bridge
the streams, He will cleave a way through the
forests, He will make my feet like hinds' feet,
and set me upon high places. I will commit myself to Him. I will hold His hand. My grasp of
His hand is weak, but His grasp of my hand is
O, so strong. He will not let me go.

# The Thirty=eighth Week.

## COURAGE.

### (Symbol, Cr.)

## Sub-Topics and Leading Texts.

September 17.—*The source of courage.* Josh. 1: 1-9. (Cr 1.)

September 18.—*Examples of courage (Old Testament).* Josh. 14:10-12. (Cr 2.)

September 19.—*Examples of courage (New Testament).* Mark 10:32-34. (Cr 3.)

September 20.—*Examples of cowardice.* Luke 22:54-62. (Cr 4.)

September 21.—*The fear of man.* Prov. 28:1. (Cr 5.)

September 22.—*Examples of the fear of man.* John 19:12, 13. (Cr 6.)

September 23.—*The fear of God.* Job 28:28. (Cr 7.)

## Texts to be Linked with the Principal Ones.

September 17.—(Cr 1.)—Deut. 20:1; 1 Sam. 17:37, 45; 2 Chron. 32:7, 8; Acts 4:13.

September 18.—(Cr 2.)—Judg. 3:31; 4:21; 7:20, 21; 1 Sam. 14:6-13; 17:32, 33; 2 Sam. 23:15, 16; Neh. 4:14; 6:10, 11; Esth. 4:16; Dan. 3:16-18; 6:10, 11.

September 19.—(Cr 3.)—Acts 5:19-21; 19:30; 20:23, 24; 21:12, 13.

September 20.—(Cr 4.)—Num. 13:31-33; Deut. 20:
    8; Judg. 15:11, 12; 1 Sam. 31:7; Matt.
    14:30; 2 Tim. 4:16.

September 21.—(Cr 5.)—Josh. 7:5; Prov. 29:25;
    Isa. 7:2; Matt. 10:28; Luke 12:4; Gal.
    1:10.

September 22.—(Cr 6.)—Ex. 32:22-24; 1 Sam. 15:
    24; 1 Kings 19:2, 3; Jer. 38:19; Matt.
    26:56, 69-74; John 12: 42, 43.

September 23.—(Cr 7.)—Deut. 4:10; 10:12, 20, 21;
    Josh. 24:14; 1 Sam. 12:14, 24; 2 Chron.
    19:7, 9; Ps. 2:11; 33:18; 34:7, 9, 11; Jer.
    32:39, 40; 2 Cor. 7:1.

## For Meditation throughout the Week.

I can do all things that God wants me to do.
He that commands me is He that strengthens me.
He has authority to command, because He has
power to strengthen. If He sends me upon a
journey, He not only marks out the way, but He
makes the way. When He bids me advance
against a foe, He not only arms me, but He hurls
before me His all-conquering thunder-bolts.
Why do I fear what men may do or say or think?
With me, if I will, is a force greater than all
armies, more majestic than all monarchies. Why
do I shrink from God's requirements? It is because I do not see God, because I see only hostile
men, or see only my own weaknesses. Let me
open my eyes to see the chariots that fill the
mountains round about me. Then shall I open
my hands to grasp my weapon, and open my
mouth to shout the battle cry: " The sword of the
Lord and of Gideon! "

# The Thirty=ninth Week.

## PATIENCE.

(Symbol, Pa.)

### Sub-Topics and Leading Texts.

September 24.—*The duty of patience.* Ps. 37:7, 8. (Pa 1.)

September 25.—*The source of patience.* Jas. 1:3. (Pa 2.)

September 26.—*The reward of patience.* Ps. 40: 1-3. (Pa 3.)

September 27.—*When to be patient.* Heb. 12:1. (Pa 4.)

September 28.—*God's patience.* Matt. 21:35-37. (Pa 5.)

September 29.—*Christ's patience.* Heb. 12:3, 4. (Pa 6.)

September 30.—*Other examples of patience.* Job 1:21. (Pa 7.)

### Texts to be Linked with the Principal Ones.

September 24.— (Pa 1.) — Eccl. 7:8; 2 Cor. 6:4; 1 Tim. 6:11; Tit. 2:2; Jas. 5:7, 8.

September 25.—(Pa 2.)—Rom. 5:3; Col. 1:11; 2 Pet. 1:6.

September 26.—(Pa 3.)—Luke 21:19; Rom. 2:7; 5: 4; 15:4; Heb. 6:12; 10:35, 36; Jas. 1:4.

September 27.—(Pa 4.)—Lam. 3:26; Matt. 18:28-30; Luke 8:15; 13:8, 9; Rom. 8:25; 12: 12; 1 Pet. 2:20.

September 28.—(Pa 5.)—Rom. 15:5.

September 29.—(Pa 6.)—Isa. 53:7; Matt. 27:14; Acts 8:32; 2 Thess. 3:5; Rev. 1:9.

September 30.—(Pa 7.)—1 Sam. 10:27; 2 Sam. 16:5-12; Heb. 6:15; Jas. 5:11; Rev. 2:2, 3.

## For Meditation throughout the Week.

How do I know God is patient with me? Because He has not destroyed me in my sins, though my sins have well deserved it. Because, continuing my life from day to day, He continues to load it with blessings. Because, in the person of His Son, He has promised patience as long as this life shall last. And shall not the contemplation of His great patience with the myriads of sinful, hateful men, inspire within me at least a little patience with my little troubles, the frets and worries of my pleasant life? Not all the woes I have endured, or could endure were my earthly life prolonged ten thousand years, would equal an instant of the sorrows God must endure from His disobedient and rebellious children. Oh, I should go with my head in the air and my heart singing for the love of God! What are my trials but mists of the morning, all to be scattered by the first daygleam of eternity?

# Tbe Fortietb Week.

## HOPE.

(Symbol, Hp.)

### Sub-Topics and Leading Texts.

October 1.—*What we hope for.* 1 Thess. 5:8. (Hp 1.)

October 2.—*Hope in God.* Ps. 71:5, 14. (Hp 2.)

October 3.—*Hope in Christ.* 1 Pet. 1:3, 13, 21. (Hp 3.)

October 4.—*Hope's effects.* Rom. 5:4, 5. (Hp 4.)

October 5.—*Hope and power.* Ps. 31:24. (Hp 5.)

October 6.—*Hope and joy.* Ps. 43:5. (Hp 6.)

October 7.—*Hope under difficulties.* Prov. 13:12. (Hp 7.)

### Texts to be Linked with the Principal Ones.

October 1.—(Hp 1.)—Ps. 33:18; 119:166; Acts 24: 15; Gal. 5:5; Tit. 1:2; 2:13; 3:7; Heb. 6:11, 18, 19.

October 2.—(Hp 2.)—Ps. 38:15; 39:7; 78:7; 130:7; Rom. 15:4, 13.

October 3.—(Hp 3.)—1 Cor. 15:19; Eph. 1:18; Col. 1:5, 23, 27; 1 Thess. 1:3; 1 Tim. 1:1.

October 4.—(Hp 4.)—Ps. 33:22; Rom. 8: 24, 25; 2 Cor. 3:12; 1 John 3:3.

October 5.—(Hp 5.)—Joel 3:16.

October 6.—(Hp 6.)—Ps. 119:74, 116; 146:5; Prov. 10:28; Jer. 17:7; Rom. 5:2; 12:12.

October 7.—(Hp 7.)—Prov. 14:32; Hos. 2:15; Acts 26:6, 7; 28:20.

### For Meditation throughout the Week.

I perceive that I have two kinds of hope. One kind fills me with unrest and thrusts confusion into my life. The other kind gives me peace that no turmoil can for an instant destroy. One kind is fluctuating, now shining like a star and now black as a cinder. The other kind glows with radiance from the very throne of God. The first is the hope I rest upon this world, and the second is the hope I have fixed in God and my Saviour. Why can I not let the false hopes go? Why can I not live in the sure things, and rejoice in steadfastness? I have made proof enough of the falsity of human ambitions. I know well enough that money does not satisfy, nor men's applause, nor ease, nor anything else I can strive for, which the markets of this earth can give. And I know that satisfaction comes from above. Lord Jesus, my hope shall be in Thee. O my God, in Thee will I put my confidence. And Thou shalt be the sum of all my desires.

# The Forty=first Week.

## HUMILITY.

### (Symbol, Hu.)

## Sub-Topics and Leading Texts.

October 8.—*The duty of humility.* Matt. 11:29. (Hu 1.)

October 9.—*The strength of humility.* Matt. 18: 2-4. (Hu 2.)

October 10.—*The rewards of humility.* Matt. 5: 3. (Hu 3.)

October 11.—*How humility is gained.* Isa. 51:1. (Hu 4.)

October 12.—*How humility is shown.* Matt. 20: 26, 27. (Hu 5.)

October 13.—*The folly of pride.* 1 Sam. 2:3. (Hu 6.)

October 14.—*The punishment of pride.* Prov. 16: 5, 18. (Hu 7.)

## Texts to be Linked with the Principal Ones.

October 8.—(Hu 1.)—Jer. 45:5; Mic. 6:8; Col. 3:12.

October 9.—(Hu 2.)—Prov. 15:33; 16:19; 1 Cor. 1: 28, 29. (Hu 2.)

October 10.—(Hu 3.)—Job. 22:29; Ps. 10:17; 25:9; Prov. 3:34; 22:4; Isa. 29:19; Luke 1:52.

October 11.—(Hu 4.)—Eccl. 5:2; Isa. 57:15; Luke 18:13, 14; Rom. 12:3, 10, 16; 1 Cor. 3:18; 13:4; Phil. 2:3.

October 12.—(Hu 5.)—Ps. 141:5; Prov. 12:15; Luke 14:10; 17:10; John 13:14–16; Eph. 4:2; 5:21.

October 13.—(Hu 6.)—Job. 25:5, 6; Ps. 8:3, 4; Rom. 7:18; 1 Cor. 10:12; 2 Cor. 3:5.

October 14.—(Hu 7.)—Ps. 9:20; Prov. 8:13; Isa. 2:11, 12; 14:12, 16; Mal. 4:1; Luke 1:51; Jas. 3:1; 1 Pet. 5:5, 6.

## For Meditation throughout the Week.

When I am weak, then am I strong. When I am strong, then am I weak indeed. My falls have ever been heralded by my pride. And what am I, that I should be proud? Or what have I done, that I should hold up my head in the presence of my God? Let me measure myself with Him and with His ideal for me, and let me cease to measure myself with men or with my own wretched achievements. It is my pride that keeps me from helping men, that puts a barrier between me and their needs. It is my pride that keeps me from learning and growing, for I go with false answers rather than seek the Teacher. It is my pride that prevents my knowing God, since only those can see Him that look upward. I will learn to think of myself as lowly as I ought to think. I will forget my good deeds, for they are not worth remembering. And I will remember Thee, O Christ.

# The Forty-second Week.

## OBEDIENCE.

### (Symbol, O.)

### Sub-Topics and Leading Texts.

October 15.—*Obeying parents.*  Ex. 20:12.  (O 1.)

October 16.—*Obeying rulers.*  Matt. 22:21.  (O 2.)

October 17.—*Obeying God.*  1 Sam. 15:22, 23.  (O 3.)

October 18.—*Rewards of obedience.*  Neh. 1:5. (O 4.)

October 19.—*Punishment of disobedience.*  Gal. 3:10.  (O 5.)

October 20.—*Examples of obedience.*  Ezra 7:10. (O 6.)

October 21.—*Examples of disobedience.*  Gen. 3: 6, 11.  (O 7.)

### Texts to be Linked with the Principal Ones.

October 15.—(O 1.)—Lev. 19:3, 32; Prov. 1:8, 9; 4:1; 6:20, 21; 10:1; 13:1; 23:22; Mal. 1: 6; Eph. 6:1-3; Col. 3:20; Heb. 12:9.

October 16.—(O 2.)—Ex. 22:28; Prov. 24:21; Eccl. 8:2; 10:20; Jer. 29:7; Matt. 17:24, 25; Acts 5:29; Rom. 13:1-7; 1 Tim. 2:1, 2; Tit. 3:1; 1 Pet. 2:13-17; 2 Pet. 2:10; Jude 8.

October 17.—(O 3.)—Deut. 4:2; 26:16; 32:46; Josh. 23:6; 1 Kings 8:61; Ezra 7:23; Eccl. 12: 13; John 14:21.

October 18.—(O 4.)—Ex. 19:5; Deut. 11:22-27; Ps. 19:11; 103:17, 18; Eccl. 8:5: Mark 3:35; John 15:10, 14; 1 John 2:17; Rev. 22:14.

October 19. — (O 5.) — Lev. 20:22; Deut. 27:26; 1 Chron. 28:9; Ps. 2:11, 12; Matt. 5:19; Jas. 2:10-12.

October 20.—(O 6.)—Gen. 6:9; Num. 9:23; 14:24; 2 Chron. 31:20, 21; Job 1:8; Matt. 9:9; Luke 1:6.

October 21.—(O 7.)—Gen. 19:26; Ex. 4:13, 14; Lev. 10:1, 2; Josh. 7:15-26; 1 Sam. 13:8-14; 15:3-28; Jonah 1:1-3.

## For Meditation throughout the Week.

Were I to see my Saviour standing before me in the full visible glory of His godhead, were I to see the lightning flash from His eyes and hear the thunder of His voice, were I to see in His nail-pierced hands the concentrated forces of all the universe, how promptly, then, and how gladly would I leap to do His slightest bidding! How would His words be treasured in my memory, lest the least of them might be overlooked! All passions, all desires, all plans and ambitions would be subordinated to that single, absorbing aim—to obey my Lord. Why should it be different just because I cannot see Him and hear Him with these eyes and ears of clay? I know that He is here. I know what His commands are. Why should I not hasten to obey them? Why should not obedience be the one purpose of my life? Let me learn to obey here in this world of probation, as I shall wish I had obeyed when I reach the world of perfect vision.

# The Forty=third Week.

## TEMPERANCE.

### (Symbol, Tm.)

### Sub-Topics and Leading Texts.

October 22.—*Temperance and power.* 1 Cor. 9: 25-27. (Tm 1.)

October 23.—*Temperance and honor.* Prov. 31: 4, 5. (Tm 2.)

October 24.—*Temperance and wisdom.* Prov. 20: 1. (Tm 3.)

October 25.—*Temperance and the future.* 1 Cor. 6: 10. (Tm 4.)

October 26.—*The way to temperance.* Tit. 2: 12. (Tm 5.)

October 27.—*Examples of drunkenness.* Gen. 9: 21. (Tm 6.)

October 28.—*The punishment of drunkenness.* Prov. 23: 20, 21, 29-35. (Tm 7.)

### Texts to be Linked with the Principal Ones.

October 22.—(Tm 1.)—Hos. 4: 11; 1 Pet. 1: 13.

October 23.—(Tm 2.)—1 Tim. 3: 2, 3, 8; Tit. 2: 2-4, 6.

October 24.—(Tm 3.)—Isa. 28: 7; Dan. 1: 3-21; Amos 6: 6.

October 25.—(Tm 4.)—Matt. 24: 48-51; Luke 21: 34; Gal. 5: 21; 1 Thess. 5: 6; 1 Pet. 4: 7.

October 26.—(Tm 5.)—Rom. 13: 13; Eph. 5: 18; 1 Thess. 5: 7, 8; 1 Pet. 5: 8; 2 Pet. 1: 6.

October 27.—(Tm 6.)—1 Sam. 25: 36; 1 Kings 16: 9; 20: 16; Esth. 1: 10, 11; Dan. 5: 1-6; Mark 6: 22.

October 28.—(Tm 7.)—Deut. 21: 20, 21; Prov. 21: 17; Isa. 5: 11, 12, 22; 28: 1, 3; Nah. 1: 10; Hab. 2: 15; 1 Cor. 5: 11.

### For Meditation throughout the Week.

To think that all over this fair earth there are at this very instant hundreds of thousands of men that are making brutes of themselves! Men that are poisoning their bodies, defacing their features, weakening their muscles, destroying their mental power. Men whose consciences are seared by the fiery liquid as with a hot iron. Men whose wives are pallid and trembling, sick at heart with a myriad woes. Men whose little children cower at their approach. Men whose poor mothers and sad fathers have no happy hour because of them. Young men, their lives thus blasted in the morning of their existence. Men in the prime of life, their usefulness turned to a mockery. Old men, their gray hairs become a crown of shame. Yes, and even blear-eyed girls and women, the synonym of heaven become a portress of hell. Can this go on, has this gone on for all these years, and the church gone on, so little moved? Must not Christ be more indignant at us than we at the saloon-keeper? What is our responsibility? What is mine?

# The Forty=fourth Week.

## PURITY.

### (Symbol, Pr.)

### Sub-Topics and Leading Texts.

October 29.—*Conscious of impurity.* Isa. 6:5, 6. (Pr 1.)

October 30.—*Symbols of purity.* Heb. 9:13, 14. (Pr 2.)

October 31.—*Pure within.* Ps. 24:3, 4. (Pr 3.)

November 1.—*The way to be pure.* 1 John 1:7, 8. (Pr 4.)

November 2.—*God, the Purifier.* Mal. 3:2, 3. (Pr 5.)

November 3.—*The gains of purity.* Matt. 5:8. (Pr 6.)

November 4.—*Pictures of purity and impurity.* 2 Pet. 2:21, 22. (Pr 7.)

### Texts to be Linked with the Principal Ones.

October 29.—(Pr 1.)—Ex. 3:4, 5; Job 25:5, 6; Prov. 20:9; 30:12; Isa. 64:6.

October 30.—(Pr 2.)—Ex. 24:8; 30:18, 19; John 13:9, 10.

October 31.—(Pr 3.)—Mic. 6:7; Matt. 23:25-28; 1 Cor. 3:16, 17; 6:19, 20; Gal. 5:16.

November 1.—(Pr 4.)—Ex. 20:14; Ps. 51:10; Dan. 3:28; John 2:14, 15; 1 Cor. 9:27; 2 Cor. 6:17, 18; Eph. 5:3, 11, 12; Phil. 4:8; 1 Tim. 5:22; 2 Tim. 2:22; Jas. 1:27; 1 John 3:3.

November 2.—(Pr 5.)—Lev. 19:2; Ps. 12:6; 19:8; 119:140; Isa. 1:18; 2 Cor. 7:1; Eph. 5:25-27; 1 Thess. 4:7.

November 3.—(Pr 6.)—2 Sam. 22:27; Job 17:9; Ps. 15:1, 2; Prov. 21:8; 22:11; Tit. 1:15.

November 4.—(Pr 7.)—Gen. 39:1-23; Prov. 6:27, 28, 32; Jas. 3:17; 1 Pet. 1:22; 2:11; Rev. 4:8; 15:6.

## For Meditation throughout the Week.

I must be pure, because God is pure. I must cast off these low thoughts of the body, or I can never hope to rise into the spiritual life. I must be pure, because without purity I can never be strong. Every impure deed, nay, every impure thought, means so much less nerve and muscle to do my work. I must be pure, because without purity I cannot be happy nor make my dear ones happy. In strength is happiness, in courage, in the ability to look men in the eye, the willingness that my life shall be disclosed, as some day it will be disclosed, before all men and angels. And I must be wholly pure. I must leave in my heart no last seed of impurity to grow and bring forth as many sins as were there before. I must not permit myself any approach to impurity, no, not so much as by a thought or a look. I must see that the wish for it is as bad for me as the deed itself. And all this I am utterly powerless to do without Thy help, O Thou Pure One! And all this, with Thy help, I can do perfectly.

# The Forty=fifth Week.

## SPEECH.

(Symbol, Sp.)

### Sub-Topics and Leading Texts.

November 5.—*The power of the tongue.* Prov. 18:21. (Sp 1.)

November 6.—*Right speaking.* Ps. 145:5-12. (Sp 2.)

November 7.—*The blessing of noble speech.* Prov. 10:11, 20, 21. (Sp 3.)

November 8.—*The curse of ignoble speech.* Job 38:2. (Sp 4.)

November 9.—*Harsh words.* Ps. 64:3, 4. (Sp 5.)

November 10.—*Swearing.* Ex. 20:7. (Sp 6.)

November 11.—*How to govern our tongues.* Prov. 15:1. (Sp 7.)

### Texts to be Linked with the Principal Ones.

November 5.—(Sp 1.)—Jas. 3:2-13.

November 6.—(Sp 2.)—Ps. 17:3; 37:30; 39:1; 71:24; 105:2; Prov. 12:22; 31:26; Eccl. 3:7; 12:11; Mal. 3:16; Col. 4:6; 1 Pet. 3:9, 10.

November 7.—(Sp 3.)—Prov. 12:18, 19, 25; 15:4; 21:23; 25:11; Isa. 50:4.

November 8.—(Sp 4.)—Ps. 70:3; Prov. 10:8, 19, 32; 12:6, 13; 13:3; 14:3; 15:14; 16:27, 28; 17:9; 18:7, 13; Matt. 12:36, 37; 1 Tim. 5:13; 2 Pet. 2:10.

November 9.—(Sp 5.)—Ps. 140:3, 11; Prov. 6:16, 19;
    25:23; 1 Cor. 6:10; Jas. 4:11; 1 Pet. 2:1.
November 10.—(Sp 6.)—Lev. 19:12; 24:16; 2 Kings
    19:22; Ps. 10:7; 59:12; 109:17, 18; 139:20;
    Jer. 23:10; Ezek. 35:12, 13; Zech. 5:3;
    Matt. 5:33–37; 12:31; 15:19; Col. 3:8;
    Jas. 5:12.
November 11.—(Sp 7.)—Judg. 8:1-3; Job. 13:5;
    Ps. 15:3; 141:3; Prov. 25:15; 26:4, 5, 20,
    21; 29:11, 20; Eccl. 5:3, 7; Matt. 5:22;
    12:34; Eph. 4:29-32; 5:4; Jas. 1:19, 26.

### For Meditation throughout the Week.

Oh marvellous tool, the tongue! A tool for Satan or for God, wherewith to fashion truth or lies, strength or weakness, happiness or misery! I have been using it carelessly. I have been using it selfishly. I have not been using it with the deliberate intention of accomplishing Christ's work with it. I have not been training it to speak His messages in the most convincing way, to plead most effectively with sinners, to comfort those that mourn, to convict those that are wayward, to counsel those that are in perplexity. I train my hands and my feet and my brain, my eyes and my ears, but I let my tongue say what it occurs to it to say. What power would be mine if I should follow out Thy will for my speech, O Christ! What power of gentle persuasion, of earnest winning, of powerful command! All this is possible for me, since Thou hast made man's mouth, and Thou art willing to guide man's words. O Lord, open Thou my lips, and my mouth shall show forth Thy praise. Amen.

# The Forty=sixth Week.

## WISDOM.

### (Symbol, Ws.)

### Sub-Topics and Leading Texts.

November 12.—*Worldly wisdom.* 1 Cor. 3: 18-20. (Ws. 1.)

November 13.—*Spiritual wisdom.* 1 Cor. 2: 15, 16. (Ws 2.)

November 14.—*The power of wisdom.* Prov. 24: 3-5. (Ws 3.)

November 15.—*The joy of wisdom.* Prov. 3: 13-24. (Ws 4.)

November 16.—*How to get wisdom.* Jas. 1: 5. (Ws 5.)

November 17.—*How to use wisdom.* 1 Pet. 3: 15. (Ws 6.)

November 18.—*How to increase wisdom.* Prov. 9: 9-11. (Ws 7.)

### Texts to be Linked with the Principal Ones.

November 12.—(Ws 1.)—Job 5: 13; Eccl. 1: 18; 12: 12; Isa. 29: 14; Jer. 8: 9; Luke 16: 8; 1 Cor. 1: 17-31; 2: 6, 7; Col. 2: 8; 1 Tim. 6: 20; Jas. 3: 15.

November 13.—(Ws 2.)—Eccl. 2: 13; 7: 12, 19; Rom. 16: 19; 1 Cor. 1: 30; Eph. 5: 17.

November 14.—(Ws 3.)—Prov. 21: 22; Eccl. 9: 13-18; 10: 10; Dan. 11: 32.

November 15.—(Ws 4.)—Prov. 4: 5-9, 13; 6: 22, 23; 8: 10, 11, 32-35; Eccl. 8: 1; Phil. 3: 8, 10.

November 16.—(Ws 5.)—1 Kings 3:12; Job 28:12–
28; Ps. 90:12; 107:43; 111:10; Prov. 2:1–
12; 7:2–4; 11:14; 16:16, 22; 23:23; 28:5;
Luke 24:45; 1 Thess. 5:21.

November 17.—(Ws 6.)—1 Kings 3:9; Job 4:3, 4;
Ps. 119:27; Prov. 15:2; 16:21, 23; Isa. 53:
11; Matt. 7:24; 25:4.

November 18.—(Ws 7.)—Prov. 1:5; 10:8, 14; Dan.
12:3, 4; Hos. 6:3; 1 Cor. 13:11; 2 Pet. 3:
18.

## For Meditation throughout the Week.

To be wise, I know, is to be strong and happy.
If I am weak and unhappy, it is because I am not
wise; and how often I *am* weak and unhappy!
Yet wisdom is possible for me. God will give it to
me, and will not upbraid. I have only to ask Him
for it. I have only to give up my own foolish pre-
tence of wisdom, and accept His wisdom that is
pure and perfect. I have only to give up the
wisdom of this world, which is foolishness with
God, and receive into a good and honest heart
the wisdom that is from above. Alas, with what
inconstancy I search for this great blessing, when
I should seek it as silver and as hidden treasure!
Henceforth it shall be my goal by day and my
desire by night. I will know no other good, I will
ask for no other blessing; it shall be my crown.
Whatever else Thou dost give me or withhold, my
Father, if Thou dost give me this, I shall be satis-
fied. For I shall be growing into Thy likeness.

# The Forty=seventh Week.

## THANKSGIVING.

### (Symbol, T.)

### Sub-Topics and Leading Texts.

November 19.—*Thanksgiving a duty.* 1 Thess. 5: 18. (T 1.)

November 20.—*Gratitude to man.* 2 Tim. 1:16–18. (T 2.)

November 21.—*Praise God!* Ps. 107:1, 2, 21, 22. (T 3.)

November 22.—*Praise to Christ and through Him.* Col. 3:17. (T 4.)

November 23.—*For what to give thanks.* 2 Cor. 9:15. (T 5.)

November 24.—*When to give thanks.* Eph. 5:20. (T 6.)

November 25.—*How to give thanks.* Prov. 3:9. (T 7.)

### Texts to be Linked with the Principal Ones.

November 19.—(T 1.)—1 Kings 8:56; 1 Chron. 29: 14; Ps. 92:1-4; 100:4; Mark 5:19; Col. 2: 7; 3:15.

November 20.—(T 2.)—Ex. 2:19, 20; Josh. 6:22–25; Ruth 1:8; 2 Sam. 10:2; 1 Kings 2:7; 2 Kings 4:13; 5:15, 16.

November 21.— (T 3.) — Ps. 50:14; 68:19; 145:7; Joel 2:26; Col. 1:12.

November 22.—(T 4.)—Rom. 1:8; Eph. 5:20; 1 Tim. 1:12; Heb. 13:15.

November 23.—(T 5.)—Deut. 26:5, 10; Ezra 7:27; Ps. 28:7; 40:2-5; 48:11; 66:1-20; 103:1-5; 147:12,13; 1 Cor. 15:57; Phil. 4:6; 1 Tim. 4:3-5.

November 24.—(T 6.)—Deut. 8:10, 18; Ps. 79:13; 89:1; Dan. 6:10; John 6:11; Rom. 14:6; Eph. 1:16; Heb. 13:15.

November 25.—(T 7.)—Gen. 32:10; 2 Sam. 7:18; Ps. 116:12-19; Isa. 48:20; 52:9; Col. 4:2.

## For Meditation throughout the Week.

How much I have to praise Thee for, O my God! My troubles are but foam floating in the ocean of my blessings. Far as I can see, they extend, wave upon wave of kindness, behind and before. Thy goodness gleams in the sunshine of Thy mercy. It bears me up as a flood. I rest in its moving arms. There is no end to it, there is no sounding of its depths. It mounts to the heavens, it covers the whole earth. And I do not deserve the least of all these benefits. Even now I am ungrateful; and because I do not at once find some fancied joy, I doubt it all. I hide my heart from the sunshine, I close my eyes to the sea. Wilt Thou send sorrow, that I may come to understand Thy blessings? Wilt Thou teach me what indeed is affliction? Thou hast been most kind to me even in this, that Thou hast not punished my ingratitude. Continue Thy forbearance, dearest Lord; for I am striving to learn my lesson, and to praise Thee as I should.

# 𝕮𝖍𝖊 𝕱𝖔𝖗𝖙𝖞=𝖊𝖎𝖌𝖍𝖙𝖍 𝖂𝖊𝖊𝖐.

## WORLDLINESS.

### (Symbol, Wr.)

### Sub-Topics and Leading Texts.

November 26.—*Worldly desires.* Eccl. 2:10, 11. (Wr 1.)

November 27.—*Worldly pleasures.* Prov. 14:13. (Wr 2.)

November 28.—*The praise of men.* John 12:43. (Wr 3.)

November 29.—*The emptiness of worldliness.* Hag. 1:6. (Wr 4.)

November 30.—*The punishment of worldliness.* Amos 6:3-7. (Wr 5.)

December 1.—*In the world but not of it.* 1 Cor. 7:31. (Wr 6.)

December 2.—*This world and the next.* 1 John 2:15-17. (Wr 7.)

### Texts to be Linked with the Principal Ones.

November 26.—(Wr 1.)—Eccl. 6:11, 12; Luke 8:14; 21:34; 1 Cor. 10:6.

November 27.—(Wr 2.)—Prov. 15:21; 27:7; Eccl. 2:1; Isa. 22:12, 13; 1 Tim. 5:6; 2 Tim. 3:4; 1 Pet. 4:3, 4.

November 28.—(Wr 3.)—1 Sam. 8:19, 20; Ps. 49:18; John 5:44; Jas. 4:4; 1 John 4:5.

November 29.—(Wr 4.)—Job 20:4, 5; 21:11-13; Eccl. 1:8; Isa. 28:4; John 4:13.

November 30.—(Wr 5.)—Ps. 106:14, 15; Isa. 24:7, 8, 11; 47:7-9; Amos 8:10; Mic. 2:10; 6:14; Phil. 3:19.

December 1.—(Wr 6.)—Ps. 4:6, 7; Matt. 6:25; 10:39; Col. 3:2; 2 Tim. 2:4; Tit. 2:12.

December 2.—(Wr 7.)—Matt. 24:38, 39; Luke 12:15-34; 16:25; 1 Pet. 1:24; 2:11.

## For Meditation throughout the Week.

I know that within a very few years I am to leave this world entirely behind me. I know that before many years, as God counts years, the world itself will pass away, crumbling back into the ether from which it came. Is it the part of a wise man or a practical man to fix my thoughts and spend my energies upon what is so empty and transient as this world's goods? Shall anything the world has to give me, or to give any one, tempt me for a moment to neglect my eternal interests? And if I am persuaded that these are safe, shall any disappointment of this world, or any trial of life, disturb the quiet happiness of my soul? I will receive this world with joy. It is a beautiful world; but its chief beauty is in its disclosures of God, and of the real things wherein God lives and would have me live. I will use this goodly world, but chiefly will I use it to prepare myself and others for the world that is to come. I will not let this thought make me visionary, but I will know through all the shifting phantasms of earth that this vision of heaven is the one solid and substantial thing, and I will fasten my life to it.

# The Forty=ninth Week.

## SORROW.

### (Symbol, So.)

## Sub-Topics and Leading Texts.

December 3.—*Sorrows as punishments.* Ps. 94: 12. (So 1.)

December 4.—*Sorrows as tests.* John 15:2. (So 2.)

December 5.—*Resignation.* 1 Thess. 3:3. (So 3.)

December 6.—*Our help in sorrow.* Deut. 33:25–27. (So 4.)

December 7.—*Peace in sorrow.* 2 Cor. 4:8–18. (So 5.)

December 8.—*Strength to endure.* Col. 1:11. (So 6.)

December 9.—*Gains from our griefs.* Matt. 5:4, 10. (So 7.)

## Texts to be Linked with the Principal Ones.

December 3.—(So 1.)—Job. 5:17; Prov. 3:11, 12; Lam. 3:29; Ezek. 20:37, 43; Hos. 5:15.

December 4.—(So 2.)—Gen. 22:12; Deut. 8:2, 3, 5, 16; Judg. 2:21, 22; Job 23:10; Ps. 66:10–12; Eccl. 7:2–4; Isa. 1:25–27; 48:10; Dan. 12:10; John 9:2, 3; 2 Cor. 12:7; Rev. 3:19.

December 5.—(So 3.)—Job. 1:21; Ps. 46:10; Eccl. 7:14; Luke 21:19; Phil. 2:14; 2 Tim. 2:3; 4:5.

December 6.—(So 4.)—Job 35: 10; Ps. 23:4; 55:22;
147:3; Isa. 41:10, 13; 42:3; 43:2; 61:1-3;
66:13; Nah.1:7; Matt.11:28; Heb. 13:5.

December 7.—(So 5.)—Ps. 126:5, 6; John 14:1, 16,
18, 27; 16:33; Rom. 8:28; Jas. 1:2-4, 12;
1 Pet. 4:12, 13, 19.

December 8.—(So 6.)—Ps. 41:3; Lam. 3:27; Rom.
5:3, 4; 2 Cor. 12:9; 2 Tim. 4:17; Heb. 12:
3; Jas. 5:11.

December 9.—(So 7.)—2 Chron. 33:12, 13; Ps. 119:
67, 71; Hos. 6:1; Luke 6:21-23; 15:17, 18;
Acts 14:22; Phil. 1:12-14; Heb. 12:5-13.

## For Meditation throughout the Week.

I will not deny sorrow, for that is not the way to
end it. The Bible does not deny it, but overcomes
it. There *are* sorrows most heavy and grievous.
The world is full of them. But there are also
alleviations, radiant, perfect. Heaven is full of
them. My heart shall be tender for the sorrows,
as Christ's was, but it shall not be despondent,
for His never was. If God sends me a grief, I
shall know that it is to chastise me for some sin,
and I will rejoice, since I am on the way to health
from the bitter medicine; or I shall know that it
is to purify me, and even in the fire I shall rejoice
in the hope that I may come forth pure gold. And
if He sends grief to my dear ones, though that is
hardest to bear of all, still I will trust in God, and
be sure that He does all things well. Blessed be
the Lord, who can give me songs in any night-
time; nay, who will open the doors of my prison
at last, and lead me out into the light.

# The Fiftieth Week.

## CHARITY.

### (Symbol, Cy.)

## Sub-Topics and Leading Texts.

December 10.—*The woes of the poor.* Prov. 10:15. (Cy 1.)

December 11.—*Oppression of the poor.* Prov. 22: 7, 22, 23. (Cy 2.)

December 12.—*The compensations of poverty.* 2 Cor. 6:10. (Cy 3.)

December 13.—*Justice to the poor.* Jer. 22:16. (Cy 4.)

December 14.—*Kindness to the poor.* Ps. 41:1-3. (Cy 5.)

December 15.—*The spirit of liberality.* Acts 20: 35. (Cy 6.)

December 16.—*God's care of the poor.* Ps. 72:2, 4, 12, 13. (Cy 7.)

## Texts to be Linked with the Principal Ones.

December 10.—(Cy 1.)—Job 30:3-6; Prov. 14:20; 30:8,9; Eccl. 9:15,16; Isa. 3:14,15; Amos 2:6-8; Jas. 2:2-4, 6.

December 11.—(Cy 2.)—Ps. 10:2, 8-10; 146:7; Prov. 18:23; 28:8; 30:14; Eccl. 5:8; Jer. 20:13; Ezek. 18:7; Zech. 7:10.

December 12.—(Cy 3.)—Ps. 113:7,8; Prov. 19:1, 22; 22:2; 28:6, 11; Eccl. 5:12; Luke 4:18; 9:58; Jas. 2:5; 1 John 3:17-19.

December 13.—(Cy 4.)—Ex. 23:6; Lev. 19:15; Ps. 82:3, 4; Prov. 29:14; Isa. 1:17.

December 14.—(Cy 5.)—Deut. 15:7-11; Job 29:11-17; 30:25; Prov. 19:17; 28:27; Eccl. 11:1; Matt. 5:42; 11:5; 25:35, 36; Mark 14:7; Luke 6:38; 14:12-14.

December 15.—(Cy 6.)—Job 31:16-22; Ps. 37:21, 26; Isa. 32:8; 58:7, 10; Matt. 6:1-4; Mark 12:43, 44; Luke 3:11; 6:35; 12:33; 18:22; Rom. 12:8, 13; 1 Cor. 13:3; 16:1, 2; 2 Cor. 9:6-12; Eph. 4:28; Jas. 2:15, 16.

December 16.—(Cy 7.)—Job 5:15, 16; Ps. 9:18; 10:14; 34:6; 35:10; 68:10; 69:33; 107:9, 36, 41; Isa. 11:4; 25:4.

## For Meditation throughout the Week.

God has given me so many good things, in part that I may enjoy having them; yes, but in part that I may enjoy giving them away. I must use my possessions, or they will possess me; and the main use of them is to make them useful to others. God wants me to increase my goods, and the most glorious increase is to put them on interest with Him, giving to the poor, lending to the Lord. God, who made all things, best knows how all things are to be enjoyed. I make a great mistake when I insist upon my own way of enjoying His gifts, and often as a result I do not enjoy them at all. Let me try God's way. It is the way He Himself enjoys whatever He has—by giving it away. Who so liberal as my God? Who gives so constantly, so unstintedly? Nay, are not all my gifts His gifts in reality? And is not this His best gift to me, to give me the power of giving?

# The Fifty=first Week.

## PATRIOTISM.

### (Symbol, Pt.)

### Sub-Topics and Leading Texts.

December 17.—*Love of country.* Isa. 66: 10, 13, 14. (Pt 1.)

December 18.—*The nation's sorrows.* Ps. 137: 1-6. (Pt 2.)

December 19.—*The nation's restoration.* Isa. 62: 1, 6, 7. (Pt 3.)

December 20.—*The nation's prosperity.* Ps. 122: 6. (Pt 4.)

December 21.—*Devotion to country.* Neh. 4: 11, 14. (Pt 5.)

December 22.—*Bible patriots.* Matt. 23: 37. (Pt 6.)

December 23.—*God and the nation.* Ps. 33: 12. (Pt 7.)

### Texts to be Linked with the Principal Ones.

December 17.—(Pt 1.)—Gen. 30: 25; 1 Kings 11: 21, 22; Ps. 102: 14.

December 18.—(Pt 2.)—Isa. 22: 4, 5; Jer. 9: 1; 14: 17.

December 19.—(Pt 3.)—Isa. 58: 12; Zech. 10: 9.

December 20.—(Pt 4.)—Job 12: 23; Ps. 20: 5, 7; 60: 4, 5, 12; 128: 5, 6; Prov. 14: 34; Isa. 9: 3; 26: 2, 15.

December 21.—(Pt 5.)—Ex. 32: 31, 32; Neh. 5: 14-18.

December 22.—(Pt 6.)—Ex. 2:11, 12; Judg. 7:18; 1 Sam. 4:13, 18; 2 Sam. 1:20; Neh. 1:2-4; 2:2, 3; Esth. 4:16.

December 23.—(Pt 7.)—Josh. 23:3; Ps. 22:27, 28; 66:7; 144:15; 147:14, 20; Isa. 2:4; 26:15; 60:12; Jer. 12:7-17; 18:7-10; Dan. 4:35; Zeph. 3:6.

## For Meditation throughout the Week.

What is this nation in which God has placed me? It is more than these vast plains, lofty mountains, and rolling rivers, more than this expanding commerce, these clashing mills, these busy streets. The nation is men and women and little children. It is the teacher that opened for me the doors of knowledge. It is my mother and my father and my dear ones. It is my wife and children. It is my home, with all its precious associations. It is memory, crowded with noble shadows. All these, and a myriad glorious things beside, my country is to me. And what am I to my country? While it is pulsing toward me with all this life and helpfulness, am I thinking of it only as of so much territory and insensate earth? Let me know henceforth that the voice of my country is truly the voice of God. Let me heed its behests almost as the commands of Deity. Let me reverence it as God's abiding-place. And let me render to it the whole-hearted service that will please the God of nations.

# The Fifty=second Week.

## PRAYER.

### (Symbol, P.)

### Sub-Topics and Leading Texts.

December 24.—*Why to pray.* Matt. 7: 7–11. (P 1.)

December 25.—*When to pray.* 1 Thess. 5: 17. (P 2.)

December 26.—*How to pray.* Matt. 6: 5–13. (P 3.)

December 27.—*For what to pray.* Luke 11: 13. (P 4.)

December 28.—*For whom to pray.* Job 42: 10. (P 5.)

December 29.—*Power in prayer.* Jas. 5: 16–18. (P 6.)

December 30.—*The answer to prayer.* Matt. 21: 22. (P 7.)

### Texts to be Linked with the Principal Ones.

December 24.—(P 1.)—1 Chron. 28: 9; Zech. 12: 10; 1 Tim. 2: 8; Heb. 4: 16.

December 25.—(P 2.)—1 Chron. 16: 11; Ps. 32: 6; 50: 15; 55: 17; Isa. 55: 6; Matt. 14: 19; Luke 18: 1, 7.

December 26.—(P 3.)—Deut. 4: 29; Prov. 16: 1, 3; Eccl. 5: 2; Jer. 29: 13; Lam. 3: 41; Hos. 14: 2; Mark 11: 25; John 4: 24; Eph. 6: 18; Heb. 11: 6; Jas. 4: 2, 3, 8.

December 27.—(P 4.)—Ps. 81: 10; Prov. 2: 3–5; Zech. 10: 1; John 14: 13, 14; 15: 7; 16: 23–27.

December 28.—(P 5.)—Num. 6: 23–26; 1 Sam. 12: 23; Ps. 122: 6; Jer. 29: 7; Joel 2: 17; Matt. 5: 44; Rom. 10: 1; Eph. 3: 14–19; 1 Tim. 2: 1, 2; Jas. 5: 14, 15.

December 29.—(P 6.)—Hos. 12: 3, 4; Acts 4: 31; Rom. 8: 26; 2 Cor. 12: 8, 9; 1 John 3: 21, 22.

December 30.—(P 7.)—Ps. 34: 15, 17; 37: 4, 5; 65: 2, 5; 145: 18, 19; Isa. 65: 24; Jer. 33: 3; Joel 2: 32; Matt. 18: 19, 20; Mark 11: 24; Eph. 3: 20; 1 John 5: 14, 15.

## For Meditation throughout the Week.

I can speak with God. I can hear Him answering me. I can be certain that He hears me. I can be sure that I hear Him. I can bring before Him a definite trouble, and go away free from it. I can ask from Him a definite petition, and I can at once give thanks, knowing that it is granted. I can come with my heart aglow with praise, and I can go away with the Father's kiss upon my brow. There is nothing in my life more real than this. It is the source of all my joy, it is the foundation of all my strength. Without it, a paradise would be a desert; with it, the most barren waste is an Eden. How do I bless Thee, O my God, for the disclosure of Thyself in Christ Jesus, my Lord! Amen.

# HINTS ON BIBLE STUDY.

THIS is called an age of Bible-study, and I will grant that it does shine conspicuous in that regard over all ages that have gone before. And yet—and yet—!

Now I am not a pessimist. But take the first Christian you come across—some regular Sunday-school scholar, say; or—take yourself. You think you are a great Bible-reader. Try it by such a test as you would give your newspaper.

"At what price did Brown and Jones offer sheeting in their advertisement?" "What page had the notice of Professor Seaver's lecture?" "What did the President say in his message?" "What was that scandal the reporter told about?—that scandal of the Thompsons, you know." Such questions as these we ask each other about our newspapers that we have read only once. And we usually get an answer.

"In what chapter and book is the saying, 'I am the light of the world'?" "Where shall I go to find out about Gideon?" "By what name did Christ most often speak of Himself?" "What is the first event mentioned in the New Testament?" "Which is the oldest book of the Bible?" Surely such questions as these ought not to trouble a regular Bible-reader, since such questions as I gave first would not trouble a hasty newspaper-reader. But just try them, and see what the result will be.

I once put into the form of an acrostic five tests of wise Bible-reading. It must be

Biblical,
Independent,
Benevolent,
Long,
Every day.

1. Your Bible-reading must be biblical. That is, you must put the Bible first. You must not read your commentary, or your Bible history, or any other book about the Bible, and think you are reading the Bible. These are all needed, but try the plan also of letting the Bible be its own commentary. When you have exhausted *its* resources, go to other books, and not till then. You will be astonished to see what depth and fulness this plan will give to your Bible knowledge.

2. Your Bible-reading must be independent. Don't go to the Bible with your head filled with other people's theories of what the Bible says; find out what it says for yourself. Don't go to it with the feeling that you *must* get from it certain doctrines. See for yourself whether those doctrines are there. No man is well indoctrinated until he has indoctrinated himself. I would not have you despise guides to Bible study,—that would be foolish. But go as far as you can by yourself. Use the methods you find most helpful. Take the order you find most convenient. It is *your* brain that is to receive; therefore it, and not the brain of another, is the judge of the way it can best follow.

3. Most Bible-study that fails, fails for want of a purpose that is adequate to carry one over its hard places. The desire to shine before men will not do it, nor will mere love of learning, nor will a barren sense of duty. Nothing will, but love of God and love of men; the desire to draw close to one's Father and help one's brother. Go to your Bible with these aims, and you will go to it with constantly increasing eagerness and profit.

4. Much Bible-reading fails because of brevity. Momentum tells in this work, as in every other. The force and beauty of large portions of the Bible can be learned only through reading several chapters at once. Ten minutes a day is far too little time for Bible-reading that shall tell; half an hour a day would allow time to get up steam, and to use the steam after it is generated. How many of you give half an hour a day to the Word of God?

5. Finally, in this brief acrostic-summary, your Bible-reading should be *every day*. It must become as much a habit as eating, and for much the same reason. You cannot eat in one day your dinners for the six following days. "Give us *day by day* our daily bread "—spiritual, as well as physical. This is one great blessing among the many that are springing from our Christian Endeavor pledge, with its promise of daily Bible-reading: it is changing for thousands their Bible-reading from a spasm into a habit. Read the Bible on the cars instead of your newspaper. Prop it up before you at your kitchen table. Put it in your pocket when you set out for a lonely walk. Be only a tenth part as zealous to get time for your Bible as you would be to get ten dollars, and you will get the time—never fear.

I have just said that your Bible-reading must be independent. True; but your independence, though good to start with, will not carry you far. You must get help from books.

The best of all book-helps for Bible-study is the Revised Version. Difficulties by the thousand are cleared up in the new version, and it places you as near as our English can to the original Hebrew and Greek. Then, don't try to get along with the concordance found in the back of the teachers' Bibles. Nothing more trying to the student was ever put within covers than these half-way compilations. They are of use only as tests of patience and good temper. On the other

116

hand, the remaining helps found in the standard teachers' Bibles are of the greatest assistance, and you will need to consult them constantly— especially the atlas. A Bible dictionary you must have, and a commentary. The best commentary in small compass is, probably, Jamieson, Faussett, and Brown's. A better plan is to buy separate commentaries on the separate books of the Bible, as you come to them in your studies. The best series of such commentaries—a series, however, as yet incomplete and its different volumes are of unequal value—is the "Cambridge Bible for Students." If you join with others in the study, the expense for books may be shared among you. These are all the books you will *need;* though, of course, the larger the library to which you have access, the better,—provided you know how to use it!

There are many ways of studying the Bible; but, manifestly, the first thing to do is to get a knowledge of its contents. Until you know what is in each book, and where to put your hand on what you want in it, no topical study can be carried on to any advantage. Straight through the Bible then, book by book, must be your first journey,—such a pilgrimage as I conduct in the companion volume to this, "A Bible Year."

Take the books in their order. First read the book. This reading will take you, in many cases, only a few minutes. Make a comprehensive survey of it. Divide it into sections, according to the changes of theme. Give titles to the chapters. Mark the most helpful passages. Commit them to memory. Write analyses of the events. Trace different characters through the book. Make a four-hundred-words abstract of the book; then a one-hundred-words abstract. Learn all you can about the author of the book, and the times in in which it was written. Geikie's "Hours with the Bible" will be of great help there. Compare the book with the books you have already studied.

Test your familiarity with the book in all sorts of ways, seeing how readily you can turn to any desired passage, seeing how much of the contents of the book you can recall in outline. Write out a set of questions on the book,—every query you can think of,—and come back to them after a few days to see whether you can answer them all. Don't leave the book for another until you are quite sure you have grasped at least its principal contents, so that you know what is in it, and where to "find things." *Then* proceed to the next book.

After you have gone through the Bible in this way, a broad and delightful field opens before you—the study of the Bible topically,—the study to which the present volume is an introduction. Each book has something to tell you about Christ. Learn what it is. There is work for many months. Trace each great doctrine through the Bible—the doctrine of immortality, of atonement, of the forgiveness of sins, of the Holy Spirit. These studies, of course, will last a lifetime, and will be as varied as the students are. It is unnecessary, and, in fact, impossible, even to outline them. My purpose is merely to insist that such topical studies should be carried out by every Christian.

A man once possessed a rare and valuable collection of medicines. This collection contained drugs from every clime, elixirs of powerful virtue, liquids of priceless worth. The owner of this noble possession often congratulated himself in the presence of his friends upon his good fortune.

"But you can't read," objected his friends.

"Nevertheless," he replied, "the collection is unequalled in the world."

"But you don't know one medicine from the other," they answered, "and if you were sick, you would only stumble in profitless confusion among all these glass bottles."

"But, don't you see?" he said, "it is mine. I own the whole matchless collection."

"No," they replied, "we don't see. You do not actually own it, though you may keep it in your house forever. No one could truly own it except a skilful physician, who could read the labels, and understand when and how to use each medicine."

Now, too many of us are in just this foolish plight regarding the Bible. We have it in our house, but not in our minds. We own the paper and binding, but the essence is not ours. *Our Bible-reading is a farce unless we practise it.*

"But how can we practise it?" you ask. "This morning I may be reading some lesson on anger, and the whole of the day may not contain a single provocation to wrath; or it may be some comforting thought regarding death, and all my dear ones are alive and in good health."

Is it not evident, then, that the only practical reading of the Bible is one that stores it away in the memory, and stores it away so systematically that any needed portion can be found just when it is needed? Of what use is a spade if it can be found only when raking is in order? What is the good of the camphor-bottle if it pops up when you need the hamamelis? What is the advantage of a handful of keys if the particular key that will fit the case is lacking?

It is not how much you read, but the manner of your reading, that counts. This is a remark so trite that you may fling it aside without seeing whether it fits you or not. A single Bible verse, digested each day and made a part of your spiritual organism, would mean in the course of the year 365 verses,—some twenty chapters. It would be easy to get the essence of the entire Bible into those 365 verses.

In this book, then, I suggest a plan for your Bible-reading. The plan is very simple. It merely consists in writing, after each Bible text you come across that is likely to be helpful, the initial of the circumstances under which it is likely to be of use. For instance, after all passages treating of death,—all passages, I mean, that appeal especially to you as you read them,—print neatly the letter D. When you meet with verses that seem to you likely to be comforting in seasons of sorrow, print after them the contraction, So. You are often worried. Place a big Hp after the many verses that help to make men hopeful. An L will distinguish for you the passages that will tend to make you a better laborer. There is little more to the plan, and the topics I have indicated, and the texts under each topic, are given merely as stimulating nuclei of your own collection, which is to grow as you grow.

This is to be a very real affair all through, and so I urge you never to mark a verse that does not at the time impress itself upon you with its beauty and force. Coming back to it some other day you may see in it a meaning you had never before suspected. Wait for that day before you mark it.

And finally, but most important point of all, *review!* Most work of this kind is a failure because it is done and then forgotten. A marked Bible is no better than an unmarked Bible unless its owner is entirely familiar with the marked passages, and can turn to any one of them whenever he pleases.

And so, as soon as you begin thus to emphasize passages, begin to review them. At first, glance over day by day every verse you have marked. Later, when the number of verses becomes larger, select each day only a single category of them, such as those marked with Ct for " contentment." Review them, and review them, until you are perfectly familiar with every verse you have marked that bears on this subject. And then, the next time you feel the cold mists of covetousness or envy settling down over your life, you will know where to go for the sunshine. To return to my former illustration, you will not put your hand on the camphor-bottle when you need the hamamelis.

# INDEX.

121

# A Bible Year

## By Amos R. Wells.

———

Every Bible - reader should own this book. It gives a complete course in Bible-reading, reading through the entire Bible in one year. In addition to the daily Bible-reading, it gives a topic for meditation every day, a daily suggestion for further study, if the reader so desires, and a brief historical account of every book in the Bible. It is very complete and yet brief. 122 pages, bound uniform with "The Bible Marksman."

**Price, 35 cents, postpaid.**

———

## United Society of Christian Endeavor,

Tremont Temple, Boston, Mass.
155 La Salle St., Chicago, Ill.